500 Amazing Facts for Kids

Table of Contents

Welcome

Hey there, adventurer! Have you ever wondered about the gigantic dinosaurs that roamed the Earth millions of years ago or the vast, mysterious space above us? What about the people and events that shaped our history? If these questions make you curious, you're in for a treat!

This book is like a treasure chest bursting with fascinating, strange, and super cool facts from history, science, and the natural world. I aim to spark your curiosity and take you on a fantastic journey through time and space, uncovering secrets and wonders that will blow your mind!

Curiosity is a powerful force that drives us to explore, learn, and grow. It pushes scientists to discover new planets, historians to uncover ancient civilizations, and kids like you to ask, "Why?" and "How?" With every page you turn, you'll feel this curiosity engine, expanding your understanding of our incredible world.

But don't worry, this isn't just another boring textbook. It's a gateway to seeing the world in a whole new way. By the end of this adventure, you'll have lots of "aha!" moments and a deeper appreciation for the mysteries and marvels that surround us every day.

So, are you ready to dive into a world of wonders? Join me on this exciting journey of discovery. Let's explore together and see the world with fresh eyes, filled with awe and wonder. Let's start this adventure, shall we?

Amazing Animals

Hey there, young explorers! Get ready to embark on a fantastic adventure where you'll meet some of the planet's most fascinating and sometimes downright weird animals. Have you ever wondered what makes a slug cool or why whales are considered the giants of the ocean? Well, you're in the right place!

In this chapter, we're diving deep into the animal kingdom, discovering incredible facts about the creatures that share our world. From the tiny but mighty insects to the majestic giants of the sea, each animal has a unique story that makes them special.

So, put on your explorer hats, grab your magnifying glasses, and set off on a journey to uncover the wonders of nature. You'll be amazed by what you learn and might even find a new favorite animal. Ready? Let's meet these marvelous creatures!

1. A chameleon's tongue can be twice the length of its body, allowing it to catch prey with lightning speed

2. Kangaroos can't walk backward. The unique structure of a kangaroo's legs and tail prevents it from moving in reverse. Their large, muscular tails provide balance and act as a third leg when hopping forward. This means they can't walk backward, as their powerful back legs, designed for jumping, do not allow backward movement. This forward-only capability is especially suited to their habitat in the open plains of Australia.

3. A cow-bison hybrid is called a "beefalo." This hybrid animal was created by crossbreeding domestic cattle with American bison (buffalo). Beefalo combines the best traits of both animals, producing leaner meat than typical cattle with bison's rich, gamey flavor. They were initially bred to improve meat production and to bring bison's hardiness to the beef industry, especially in areas with harsh climates.

4. Hummingbirds are the only birds that can fly backward. These tiny birds have unique ball-and-socket joints at the shoulder, allowing their wings to rotate 180 degrees in all directions. This extraordinary flexibility enables them to hover, fly sideways, and even backward, which is particularly useful when navigating around flowers to feed on nectar.

5. A group of flamingos is called a "flamboyance." Flamingos are known for their vibrant pink feathers, which they get from the carotenoid pigments in their diet of algae and crustaceans. When

gathered together, their striking appearance and synchronized movements in large flocks create a dazzling visual display, aptly referred to as a pretension.

6. Elephants are the only animals that can't jump. Due to their enormous size and weight, elephants have evolved a unique skeletal structure that supports their massive bodies. Compared to other animals, their legs are more column-like, providing stability but lacking the springy tendons necessary for jumping. Instead, elephants rely on their strength and endurance to navigate their environment.

7. Slugs have four noses. Each pair of tentacles on a slug's head serves a different purpose: the upper pair contains light sensors, while the lower pair is responsible for smelling and tasting. These sensory organs help slugs navigate their environment, find food, and detect danger, making them highly efficient despite their simple appearance.

8. Giraffes have the same number of neck vertebrae as humans – seven. Despite their long necks, giraffes and humans share the same cervical vertebrae. However, each vertebra in a giraffe's neck can be over 10 inches long, providing the necessary length and flexibility for reaching high foliage and performing their distinctive necking battles during mating season.

9. A group of owls is called a "parliament." This term likely originates from the depiction of owls as wise and knowledgeable creatures reminiscent of a governing body. The collective noun adds a touch of whimsy to our understanding of these nocturnal birds.

10. Some cats are allergic to humans. Just as people can be allergic to cats, the reverse is true. Though rare, some cats can have allergic reactions to human dander, making them sneeze or develop skin irritations.

11. You can hear a blue whale's heartbeat from over two miles away. The blue whale's heart is so powerful that its beats can be

detected from a significant distance. This fact underscores the immense size and strength of the world's largest animal.

12. A species of ant only lives in a small area of New York City. Dubbed the "ManhattAnt," this ant was discovered in a specific urban environment and has adapted to its unique habitat, showcasing the adaptability and diversity of ant species.

13. Starfish can regrow lost arms; sometimes, a new starfish can grow from a single lost arm. This remarkable regenerative ability allows starfish to recover from injuries and produce new individuals from severed limbs, showcasing their resilience and adaptability.

14. Butterflies taste with their feet. When a butterfly lands on a plant, sensory hairs on its feet, known as tarsi, help it determine whether the plant is suitable for laying eggs or providing nectar. These chemoreceptors can detect sugar, salts, and other chemicals, allowing the butterfly to make quick and effective decisions about its food sources and breeding sites.

15. Cows have best friends and can become stressed when they are separated. Studies have shown that cows form close bonds with specific members of their herd and can experience stress and anxiety when these bonds are broken. These social animals often spend their time grazing and resting with their preferred companions, demonstrating that even livestock have complex social structures and emotional needs.

16. The heart of a blue whale is as big as a small car, weighing around 1,500 pounds. This heart is a testament to the sheer size of the largest animal on Earth. It pumps approximately 220 liters of blood with each beat, ensuring oxygen and nutrients are distributed throughout its colossal body. Blue whales can grow up to 100 feet in length and weigh as much as 200 tons.

17. A snail can sleep for three years. Snails are known for their slow pace and unique ability to enter extended periods of hibernation, known as estivation, to survive unfavorable conditions. During

this time, they seal themselves off in their shells with a layer of mucus to retain moisture and protect against predators. They are conserving energy until conditions improve.

18. Polar bears have black skin and transparent fur. Their black skin absorbs heat from the sun, while their transparent fur reflects and scatters light, making them appear white and providing excellent camouflage in their snowy Arctic habitat. This combination of physical traits helps them stay warm and hunt effectively in one of the planet's most extreme environments.

19. Some sea snakes can breathe through their skin. Certain species of sea snakes have adapted to their aquatic environment by developing the ability to absorb oxygen directly through their skin, particularly around their heads. This adaptation allows them to remain submerged while hunting for prey, reducing the need to surface frequently for air.

20. A rhinoceros' horn is made of hair. Unlike the horns of other animals, typically made of bone, a rhino's horn is composed of keratin, the same protein found in human hair and nails. This densely packed hair-like structure gives the horn strength and durability, making it a formidable tool for defense and dominance displays.

21. Ostriches can run faster than horses. With powerful legs and a speed of around 60 miles per hour, ostriches are the fastest-running birds on land. Their legs are strong and highly efficient, allowing them to cover great distances at high speeds. This ability helps them escape predators in their native African savannas.

22. Starfish or sea stars have no brains. Despite lacking a central brain, they have a complex nervous system that allows them to perform various functions such as moving, eating, and sensing their environment. Their bodies are equipped with radial nerves extending from a central nerve ring, which coordinate their movements and responses to stimuli.

23. Sea otters hold hands while sleeping to avoid drifting apart. This adorable behavior, known as rafting, ensures that sea otters remain close to each other while resting in the water. They create a "raft" that keeps them together by holding hands or wrapping themselves in kelp, reducing the risk of separation by currents and waves.

24. Honeybees can recognize human faces. Using configural processing, honeybees can distinguish between human faces by identifying the spatial arrangement of facial features. This remarkable ability helps them navigate complex environments and remember the locations of essential resources, demonstrating their advanced cognitive capabilities.

25. Pigeons can be trained to play ping-pong. Through training sessions involving rewards and conditioning, pigeons have been taught to perform various tasks, including playing a simplified version of ping-pong. This ability to learn and respond to stimuli highlights the intelligence and adaptability of these often underestimated birds.

26. Cows produce more milk when they listen to music. Studies have shown that soothing music for cows can reduce stress levels and increase milk production. The calming effects of music help create a more relaxed environment, which can lead to happier and healthier cows that produce more milk.

27. A lion's roar can be heard up to 5 miles away. Lions have incredibly powerful vocal cords, allowing their roars to travel long distances. This impressive vocalization helps them communicate with other pride members, establish territory, and deter potential threats. The ability to roar is crucial for maintaining social bonds and ensuring the group's safety.

28. Sharks have existed for longer than trees. Fossil evidence indicates that sharks existed for over 400 million years, predating the first trees by about 50 million years. These ancient predators have evolved to become highly efficient hunters, with

adaptations that have allowed them to survive and thrive in various marine environments throughout Earth's history.

29. An octopus has blue blood. This blue color comes from a copper-based molecule called hemocyanin, which is more efficient than hemoglobin at transporting oxygen in cold and low-oxygen environments. This adaptation allows octopuses to thrive in the deep ocean, with low temperatures and limited oxygen levels.

30. Dogs' sense of smell is 40 times better than humans. Dogs have up to 300 million olfactory receptors in their noses, compared to about 6 million in humans. This exceptional sense of smell allows them to detect a wide range of scents, from tracking scents over long distances to identifying medical conditions such as cancer or diabetes in humans.

31. Butterflies can see ultraviolet light. While humans can only see a limited spectrum of colors, butterflies can perceive ultraviolet light, which helps them find nectar-rich flowers and potential mates. Many flowers have ultraviolet patterns that guide butterflies to their nectar, which is invisible to the human eye.

32. The longest recorded flight of a chicken is 13 seconds. Despite being primarily ground-dwelling birds, chickens can fly short distances. Their flights are typically limited to escaping predators or reaching roosting spots, but some chickens have demonstrated impressive bursts of flight, covering up to 200 feet in the process.

33. Komodo Dragons' Asexual Reproduction: Komodo dragons have a remarkable reproductive adaptation known as parthenogenesis, allowing females to lay eggs without mating. This capability enables Komodo dragons to produce offspring even in the absence of a male, ensuring their survival in isolated environments where finding a mate might be challenging.

34. Box Jellyfish's Complex Eyes: Box jellyfish have 24 eyes, an extraordinary feature that includes eyes capable of detecting color and others that sense light. These specialized eyes help

them navigate their underwater environment effectively, avoiding obstacles and detecting prey with impressive precision.

35. Male Seahorses Giving Birth: In a unique reversal of traditional reproductive roles, male seahorses carry and breed offspring. The female deposits her eggs into a specialized pouch on the male's abdomen, where he fertilizes and incubates them until they hatch, giving birth to fully formed miniature seahorses.

36. Tarantulas' Limb Regeneration: Tarantulas possess an incredible ability to regrow lost limbs. If a tarantula loses a leg, it can regenerate it during subsequent molts, a process that showcases their remarkable regenerative capabilities and aids in their survival in the wild.

37. Electric Eels' Shocking Ability: Electric eels have specialized cells called electrocytes that enable them to generate powerful electric shocks of up to 600 volts. These shocks stun prey or defend against predators, making electric eels formidable hunters and unique among aquatic creatures.

38. A Group of Jellyfish Called a "Smack": When jellyfish gather in large numbers, they form a group known as a "smack." This term reflects the visual impact of a large congregation of these gelatinous marine animals, creating an awe-inspiring spectacle in the ocean.

39. There is an immortal species of jellyfish. The Turritopsis dohrnii, also known as the "immortal jellyfish," has the unique ability to revert its cells to an earlier stage of development when injured or threatened.

40. Archerfish are skilled hunters known for their ability to shoot water jets with impressive accuracy. They use this technique to knock insects off overhanging branches into the water, where they can be easily caught and consumed.

41. Emperor penguins are the tallest and heaviest of all penguin species, reaching heights of up to 4 feet and weighing about 100

pounds. Their large size and robust build make them well-suited to endure the harsh conditions of their Antarctic habitat.

42. Mantis shrimp possess the fastest punch in the animal kingdom, capable of striking with the speed of a bullet. This powerful punch can break glass aquarium walls and stun or kill prey, demonstrating their remarkable predatory abilities.

43. Wombats' Cube-Shaped Poop: Wombats produce cube-shaped feces, a unique trait thought to prevent their droppings from rolling away. This helps wombats effectively mark their territory, and the distinctive shape results from their digestive system's structure and slow digestion process.

44. he mimic octopus can change its color and shape to imitate more dangerous sea creatures, such as lionfish and snakes. This clever mimicry helps the octopus avoid predators by appearing as a more threatening animal, showcasing its adaptability and intelligence.

45. Axolotls are remarkable amphibians known for their ability to regenerate limbs, spinal cords, hearts, and other organs. This extraordinary capability makes them a valuable subject of scientific research, with potential implications for regenerative medicine.

46. Tardigrades, also known as water bears, can survive extreme conditions lethal to most other organisms. These microscopic creatures can endure freezing temperatures, intense radiation, and even the vacuum of space, showcasing their incredible resilience.

47. A Group of Porcupines Called a "Prickle": When porcupines gather together, they form a group known as a "prickle." This fitting name reflects the defensive nature of these spiny rodents, which are well-protected by their sharp quills.

48. Due to their genetic similarity to humans, gorillas can catch many of the same diseases, such as colds and other respiratory infections. This vulnerability significantly threatens gorilla

populations, especially where human-wildlife interactions are common.

49. A shrimp's heart is in its head. Specifically, it is located in the thorax, part of the cephalothorax, a section that combines the head and the thorax. This anatomical feature is just one of many fascinating aspects of shrimp biology.

50. If you lift a kangaroo's tail off the ground, it can't hop. A kangaroo's tail acts as a counterbalance and a third leg, providing stability and propulsion when hopping. Without the support of its tail, a kangaroo loses its balance and cannot effectively move forward. This reliance on the tail highlights the unique adaptations that enable kangaroos to navigate their environment efficiently.

51. A blue whale's tongue can weigh as much as an elephant; the largest animal on Earth, the blue whale, has a tongue that can weigh up to 2.7 tons (5,400 pounds). This massive tongue helps the whale consume up to 4 tons of krill per day during feeding season, supporting its enormous size and energy requirements.

52. Sea cucumbers can eject their internal organs to scare off predators. When threatened, sea cucumbers expel their intestines and other internal organs, which can be toxic or distasteful to predators. This defense mechanism allows them to escape while the predator is distracted. Sea cucumbers can regenerate their lost organs over time, demonstrating their resilience and adaptability.

53. Sloths can hold their breath longer than dolphins can. Sloths can slow their heart rate and metabolism to conserve energy, allowing them to have their breath for up to 40 minutes. In contrast, dolphins typically hold their breath for about 10 minutes while diving. This remarkable ability helps sloths survive in their slow-paced, tree-dwelling lifestyle.

54. An octopus has nine brains. Each of the eight arms has its own mini-brain or ganglion, that controls movement and sensory

input. This complex nervous system allows octopuses to perform intricate tasks and exhibit remarkable problem-solving abilities.

55. Male lions can sleep up to 20 hours daily. This extensive rest period allows them to conserve energy for hunting and protecting their pride, which requires significant physical exertion.

56. Crows are incredibly intelligent birds, capable of using tools, recognizing human faces, and planning for the future. Their problem-solving abilities and adaptability make them one of the most intelligent avian species, with complex social behaviors and communication skills.

57. Male platypuses have spurs on their hind legs that can deliver venom. This venom is primarily used during fights with other males, especially during the breeding season, to establish dominance and secure mating opportunities.

58. The aye-aye is a unique primate with an elongated middle finger used to tap on trees and locate insects hiding inside. Once it detects its prey, the aye-aye uses the same finger to extract the insects, showcasing its specialized feeding adaptation.

59. Cuttlefish can rapidly change their skin color and texture to blend in with their surroundings or communicate with other cuttlefish. This remarkable ability helps them avoid predators, hunt prey, and interact with other specifics in their complex underwater environment.

60. Male penguins often present a pebble to a female during courtship to symbolize their intention to build a nest together. This romantic gesture is crucial in penguin mating rituals and strengthens pair bonds.

61. The immortal jellyfish, Turritopsis dohrnii, can revert to its juvenile form after reaching maturity. This ability to effectively transform its cells into an earlier stage allows it to bypass death, making it a unique and fascinating organism in the animal kingdom.

62. Koalas have fingerprints that are almost identical to those of humans. These unique prints can sometimes be mistaken for human fingerprints at crime scenes, highlighting the close evolutionary relationship between koalas and primates.

63. Octopuses can taste with their arms. The suckers on an octopus's arms contain chemoreceptors that allow them to taste and feel their environment, enhancing their ability to hunt and explore.to meet some of our planet's most fascinating and sometimes weird animals! From cool slugs to majestic whales, discover amazing facts about the incredible creatures we share our world with.

As we wrap up our exploration of the fascinating and sometimes weird animals that inhabit our world today, it's amazing to think about how diverse and unique life on Earth is. From the tiny, colorful slugs to the majestic giants of the oceans, each creature has a story that adds to the rich tapestry of our planet's history. But our journey doesn't stop here. Now, we're about to take a giant leap back in time to discover some of the most incredible creatures that ever lived: the dinosaurs.

Imagine what our world was like millions of years ago, long before humans appeared. The landscape was vastly different, with strange and gigantic plants, and the skies and seas were filled with creatures unlike anything we see today. This was the Age of Dinosaurs, a time when these colossal beasts roamed the Earth. While our modern animals are captivating, the dinosaurs hold a special place in the annals of natural history, offering a glimpse into a world that has long since vanished.

Transitioning from the vibrant and diverse animal kingdom of today to the ancient world of dinosaurs allows us to appreciate the evolutionary journey that life on Earth has undergone. By studying dinosaurs, we can understand more about how life adapts, survives, and thrives through the ages. So, get ready to leave the present behind as we travel back to a time when the ground shook with the footsteps of giants and the air echoed with the calls of creatures long extinct. Welcome to the world of dinosaurs, where our adventure continues!

Dangerous Dinosaurs

Hey there, young explorers and budding paleontologists! We're about to embark on an exciting journey back in time to a world where colossal dinosaurs roamed the Earth. Imagine stepping into a time machine and finding yourself surrounded by towering giants and fierce predators. These ancient creatures are some of the coolest characters in our planet's history, and there's still so much to learn about them. Are you ready to become a dinosaur detective? Let's dive in!

Dinosaurs lived millions of years ago, long before humans walked the Earth. They came in all shapes and sizes, from the small and speedy Velociraptor to the gigantic and gentle Brachiosaurus. Each species had its own unique features and adaptations that helped it survive in a prehistoric world that was both beautiful and brutal. As dinosaur detectives, we'll explore the fascinating lives of these creatures, uncovering clues about their behavior, diet, and habitats.

One of the most thrilling aspects of studying dinosaurs is that new discoveries are constantly being made. Paleontologists, the scientists who study fossils, are like real-life detectives. They dig up bones, teeth, and even footprints, piecing together the mysteries of how dinosaurs lived and died. With each new fossil find, we learn a little more about these magnificent creatures. Who knows? Maybe one day, one of you will make a groundbreaking discovery that changes our understanding of dinosaurs forever!

Did you know that some dinosaurs had feathers? Or that some were covered in scales, while others had bony armor? Dinosaurs were incredibly diverse, and their physical characteristics were just as varied as the environments they lived in. From dense forests and swamps to vast deserts, dinosaurs adapted to their surroundings in amazing ways. We'll take a closer look at some of the most famous dinosaurs, as well as a few that are less well-known but just as fascinating.

So, grab your magnifying glasses and fossil brushes, and get ready for a prehistoric adventure! We'll uncover the secrets of the mighty T-Rex, learn about the long-necked giants, and even meet some flying reptiles. Whether you're a fan of the fierce carnivores or the gentle herbivores, this journey through the Age of Dinosaurs will be filled with wonder and excitement. Let's step back in time and discover the incredible world of dinosaurs together!

64. The term "dinosaur" means "terrible lizard." Coined by Sir Richard Owen in 1842, it is derived from the Greek words "deinos," meaning terrible, and "sauros," meaning lizard. Despite their reptilian name, dinosaurs were diverse creatures that dominated the Earth for over 160 million years during the Mesozoic Era.

65. The largest dinosaur ever discovered is Argentinosaurus. This titanosaur was an enormous herbivore that roamed South America during the Late Cretaceous period. Estimates suggest it could reach lengths of up to 100 feet (30 meters) and weigh as much as 100 tons, making it one of the largest land animals ever lived.

66. Tyrannosaurus rex had a bite force of up to 12,000 pounds per square inch. This incredible power allowed T. rex to crush bones and consume even the most challenging parts of its prey. Its strong jaw muscles and serrated teeth made it one of the most formidable predators of the Late Cretaceous period.

67. Dinosaurs are more closely related to birds than to reptiles. Modern birds are considered avian dinosaurs, having evolved from theropod ancestors. Features such as feathers, hollow bones, and specific skeletal structures link birds directly to their dinosaurian lineage, bridging the gap between these ancient creatures and contemporary avian species.

68. Some dinosaurs had feathers. Fossil evidence has revealed that many theropod dinosaurs, including Velociraptor and Sinosauropteryx, had feathers. These feathers were likely used for display, insulation, and, in some cases, aiding in flight or gliding. The discovery of feathered dinosaurs has significantly changed our understanding of their appearance and behavior.

69. The smallest known dinosaur is the Microraptor. This tiny, four-winged dinosaur lived about 120 million years ago during the Early Cretaceous period. Microraptor measured around 2.5 feet (0.76 meters) in length and weighed only about 2.2 pounds (1 kilogram). Its small size and feathered limbs suggest it could glide or even powered flight.

70. Stegosaurus had a brain the size of a walnut. Despite its large body, which could grow up to 30 feet (9 meters) long, this herbivorous dinosaur had a tiny brain. This brain was roughly the size of a walnut, weighing only about 2.8 ounces (80 grams). Its

brain size suggests that Stegosaurus had relatively simple behavior compared to other dinosaurs.

71. Triceratops had over 800 teeth in its lifetime. This iconic herbivore had a constantly replenishing supply of teeth arranged in groups called dental batteries. As teeth wore down from grinding plant material, new teeth would grow in to replace them. This efficient dental system helped Triceratops process thorny vegetation.

72. Some dinosaurs had built-in armor. Ankylosaurs, such as Ankylosaurus, were heavily armored dinosaurs covered in bony plates and spikes. These herbivores also had large, club-like tails that they could use to defend themselves against predators. Their formidable armor made them challenging targets for even the most ferocious carnivores.

73. Pterosaurs were not dinosaurs but flying reptiles. Often mistaken for dinosaurs, pterosaurs were a distinct group of flying reptiles that lived alongside dinosaurs. Their wings were made of a membrane stretched between their elongated fourth finger and body. Pterosaurs ranged in size from small species with wingspans of a few feet to giants like Quetzalcoatlus, with wingspans over 30 feet (9 meters).

74. Brachiosaurus had longer front legs than back legs. This unique feature gave Brachiosaurus a giraffe-like posture, allowing it to reach high vegetation. Brachiosaurus's long front legs and neck helped it access food sources that other herbivores couldn't reach, unlike most other sauropods, which had relatively equal limb lengths.

75. Some dinosaurs had crests or horns for display or combat. Dinosaurs like Parasaurolophus had elaborate crests on their heads, while others, such as Ceratosaurus, had prominent horns. These features were likely used for various purposes, including species recognition, attracting mates, and intimidating rivals or predators.

76. Oviraptors were named "egg thieves" but were caring parents. Initially believed to have been stealing eggs due to their fossilized remains being found near nests, Oviraptors were later understood to be brooding their own eggs. This misconception was corrected when better-preserved fossils showed Oviraptors in protective postures over their nests.

77. Dinosaurs lived on every continent, including Antarctica. Fossil discoveries have revealed that dinosaurs inhabited a wide range of environments across the globe. During the Mesozoic Era, the continents were arranged differently, forming the supercontinent Pangaea, which allowed dinosaurs to spread and diversify into various ecological niches.

78. The Velociraptor was much smaller than depicted in movies. Contrary to its portrayal in films like Jurassic Park, the Velociraptor was about the size of a turkey, measuring around 6 feet (1.8 meters) long and weighing about 30 pounds (14 kilograms). Despite its small size, the Velociraptor was a formidable predator with sharp claws and keen intelligence.

79. Hadrosaurs are known as "duck-billed" dinosaurs. These herbivorous dinosaurs had flat, broad beaks similar to modern ducks, which they used to strip leaves and vegetation. Hadrosaurs like Maiasaura and Edmontosaurus were highly successful and widespread, with complex social behaviors and nesting habits.

80. Some dinosaurs had exceptionally long necks. Sauropods like Diplodocus and Mamenchisaurus had necks reaching up to 50 feet (15 meters) long. These long necks allowed them to feed on vegetation high in trees or low to the ground without moving their massive bodies, providing an efficient way to consume large amounts of food.

81. Spinosaurus was one of the largest carnivorous dinosaurs. It lived during the Cretaceous period and could grow up to 59 feet (18 meters) long. It had a distinctive sail on its back and adaptations for a semi-aquatic lifestyle, including paddle-like feet and a crocodile-like snout for catching fish.

82. Iguanodon had thumb spikes. One of the first dinosaurs to be discovered and scientifically described, Iguanodon had large thumb spikes that were likely used for defense against predators. These spikes could deliver powerful blows, making Iguanodon a challenging target for carnivorous dinosaurs.

83. Some dinosaurs, like Therizinosaurus, had enormous claws that could grow up to 3 feet (1 meter) long. These claws were likely used for foraging and defense rather than hunting. Despite its fearsome appearance, Therizinosaurus was an herbivore that fed on plants and vegetation.

84. The first dinosaur fossil was discovered in the early 19th century. In 1824, William Buckland described the first scientifically recognized dinosaur, Megalosaurus. This discovery marked the beginning of paleontology as a formal science and sparked widespread interest in studying ancient life.

85. Some dinosaurs lived in herds. Evidence from fossilized footprints and bone beds suggests that many dinosaurs, such as hadrosaurs and ceratopsians, lived in large social groups. Living in herds provided protection from predators and allowed for more efficient foraging and care of the young.

86. Dinosaurs had diverse diets. While many dinosaurs were herbivores, others were carnivores or omnivores. Their diets varied widely, with some feeding on plants, insects, small animals, or other dinosaurs. This dietary diversity allowed dinosaurs to occupy various ecological niches and thrive in different environments.

87. The asteroid's impact that caused the dinosaurs' extinction created the Chicxulub Crater. Approximately 66 million years ago, a massive asteroid struck the Yucatán Peninsula in Mexico, creating the Chicxulub Crater. This impact caused widespread fires, tsunamis, and a "nuclear winter" effect, leading to the extinction of about 75% of Earth's species, including most dinosaurs.

88. Some dinosaurs could run at speeds of up to 40 miles per hour. Dinosaurs like the agile Ornithomimus were built for speed, with long legs and lightweight bodies. Their adaptations allowed them to dash to escape predators or chase down prey, demonstrating the incredible diversity of locomotive strategies among dinosaurs.

89. The Triassic Period lasted about 50 million years. It began approximately 250 million years ago and ended around 200 million years ago, marking the start of the Mesozoic Era and the age of dinosaurs.

90. The Jurassic Period lasted about 56 million years. It began around 200 million years ago and ended about 144 million years ago. It was characterized by the dominance of giant sauropods and the diversification of many other dinosaur species.

91. The Cretaceous Period lasted about 79 million years. Starting around 144 million years ago and ending approximately 65 million years ago, this period saw the peak of dinosaur diversity and the appearance of flowering plants.

92. Some dinosaurs were adapted to life in water or semi-aquatic environments. Notable among them is the Spinosaurus, which had paddle-like feet and a crocodile-like snout ideal for catching fish. These adaptations indicate that Spinosaurus spent significant time in aquatic habitats, hunting and thriving in a niche quite different from most terrestrial relatives.

93. Allosaurus, a formidable predator from the Late Jurassic period, possessed a remarkably flexible jaw. This anatomical feature allowed Allosaurus to open its mouth extremely wide, enabling it to take large, powerful bites of its prey. Such adaptability would have given it a significant advantage in tackling and consuming large herbivorous dinosaurs of its time.

94. "Velociraptor" translates to "swift thief," aptly describing this agile and cunning predator. Known for its speed and hunting prowess, the Velociraptor was a small but highly effective hunter,

capable of quick, coordinated attacks that made it a formidable foe despite its size.

95. Pachycephalosaurus is distinguished by its thick, domed skull, which could be up to 10 inches thick. This unique feature likely played a role in head-butting during combat or mating rituals. It is a weapon and a display structure to assert dominance or attract mates within its species.

96. Ankylosaurus was one of the most heavily armored dinosaurs, featuring a large, club-like tail. This tail served as a potent defensive weapon against predators, delivering powerful blows to deter or incapacitate attackers. Its armored body and tail club made Ankylosaurus a well-protected herbivore in the Late Cretaceous period.

97. Diplodocus, a long-necked herbivore, had a distinctive whip-like tail that may have served multiple purposes. This long, flexible tail could have been used to defend against predators, communicate with other dinosaurs, or even create loud cracking sounds as a display or deterrent mechanism.

98. Tyrannosaurus rex, one of the most famous theropods, had two-fingered hands, unlike many others with three or more fingers. These robust and muscular hands likely aided in grasping prey, supporting the T. rex's role as a dominant predator in the Late Cretaceous ecosystem.

99. "Stegosaurus" means "roofed lizard," a reference to the large, flat plates along its back. These plates may have been used for display to attract mates, thermoregulation to control body temperature, or defense against predators by making the dinosaur appear larger and more intimidating.

100. Maiasaura, meaning "good mother lizard," exhibited complex social behavior, including caring for its young. Fossil evidence shows that Maiasaura built nests and looked after their hatchlings, providing protection and care, which indicates a high

level of parental investment and social interaction among these dinosaurs.

101. The largest dinosaur eggs ever discovered are about 18 inches long and are believed to belong to a titanosaur. These eggs in Argentina provide insight into the reproductive strategies and development of some of the largest dinosaurs.

102. Camarasaurus, a large sauropod, had hollow spaces in its vertebrae, making its massive bones lighter. This adaptation helped support its enormous size without becoming overly heavy, allowing for efficient movement and reducing the energy required for locomotion.

103. Parasaurolophus is known for its long, curved cranial crest, which may have been used to produce sounds for communication, attract mates, or recognize other members of its species. The crest's complex internal structure likely acted as a resonance chamber, amplifying vocalizations.

104. Ornithomimids like Gallimimus resembled modern ostriches with long legs and beaks. These dinosaurs were likely speedy runners, using their agility to escape predators and perhaps to chase down prey or forage effectively.

105. Carnotaurus, a large theropod, had tiny vestigial arms compared to its body size. Unlike other predators that used their arms for hunting, Carnotaurus relied more on its powerful jaws and speed, with its tiny arms playing little to no role in its predatory lifestyle.

106. Amargasaurus had two rows of long spines running along its neck and back. These spines may have supported a sail-like structure or served for display or defense, making Amargasaurus a distinctive and visually striking dinosaur.

107. Mosasaurus was a giant marine reptile that lived during the Late Cretaceous period. As a powerful swimmer, it dominated the oceans, preying on fish, squid, and other aquatic reptiles. This showcases the diversity of reptile life during the age of dinosaurs.

108. Plateosaurus was one of the first large herbivorous dinosaurs to live during the Late Triassic period. With its long neck and robust body, Plateosaurus could reach vegetation high up in trees, setting the stage for the later development of even larger sauropods.

109. Pterodactylus, one of the earliest known pterosaurs, lived alongside dinosaurs but was not a dinosaur. It was an agile flier with a wingspan of about 3 feet, highlighting the early evolution of flying reptiles in the Mesozoic era.

110. Hadrosaurus was the first dinosaur described in North America, and its fossils were discovered in New Jersey in 1858. It was also the first nearly complete dinosaur skeleton found on the continent, providing a significant leap in paleontological knowledge and understanding of dinosaurs.

111. Stygimoloch's Spiked Skull: Stygimoloch, a pachycephalosaurid dinosaur, had a spiked, dome-shaped skull. With bony spikes and nodules, this distinctive feature may have been used in head-butting contests or as a display structure to attract mates or intimidate rivals.

112. Cryolophosaurus, the Frozen Crested Lizard: Cryolophosaurus, known as the "frozen crested lizard," was discovered in Antarctica. It lived during the Early Jurassic period, and its discovery demonstrates that dinosaurs inhabited a variety of climates, including the cold polar regions.

113. The average lifespan of dinosaurs varied widely. Large herbivorous dinosaurs like sauropods might have lived for up to 100 years, benefiting from their size and slower metabolisms. In contrast, smaller theropods likely had shorter lifespans, similar to modern birds and reptiles.

114. Ichthyosaurs, the Marine Reptiles: Ichthyosaurs were marine reptiles that resembled modern dolphins. They lived during the Mesozoic Era and were highly adapted to life in the ocean, with streamlined bodies and powerful tails for swift swimming.

115. Herrerasaurus, the Ancient Predator: Herrerasaurus is one of the oldest known dinosaurs, dating back about 230 million years to the Late Triassic period. This early carnivorous dinosaur provides crucial insights into the early stages of dinosaur evolution and diversification.

116. The Utahraptor is one of the largest raptors ever discovered, measuring about 20 feet long. Equipped with large, sickle-shaped claws on its feet, Utahraptor was a formidable predator, showcasing the diversity and adaptability of theropod dinosaurs.

117. Psittacosaurus, an early ceratopsian from the Early Cretaceous period, had a parrot-like beak. This specialized beak allowed it to eat tough, thorny plants, highlighting the dietary adaptations of herbivorous dinosaurs.

118. Giganotosaurus was one of the largest carnivorous dinosaurs, rivaling Tyrannosaurus rex in size. Living in South America during the Late Cretaceous period, it was a dominant predator, emphasizing the global diversity of large theropods.

119. Quetzalcoatlus was one of the largest flying animals of all time, with a wingspan of up to 36 feet. This Late Cretaceous pterosaur demonstrates the incredible size and adaptability of flying reptiles, pushing the limits of vertebrate flight.

120. Nigersaurus, a sauropod dinosaur, had a broad, straight-edged mouth lined with hundreds of tiny teeth. This unique adaptation allowed it to graze on low-lying vegetation like a vacuum cleaner, illustrating the diverse feeding strategies of herbivorous dinosaurs.

121. Coelophysis, one of the earliest known theropods, lived during the Late Triassic period. Measuring about 10 feet long, it was a swift and agile predator, providing insights into the early evolution of carnivorous dinosaurs.

122. Eoraptor, living around 231 million years ago during the Late Triassic period in Argentina, is considered one of the earliest

dinosaurs. Its small, bipedal form offers a glimpse into the initial stages of dinosaur evolution and diversification.

123. Early fossil discoveries in China were often mistaken for dragon bones. These ancient interpretations highlight how prehistoric remains were integrated into local mythology and folklore before the advent of modern paleontology.

124. The discovery of Archaeopteryx in 1861 provided critical evidence for the connection between dinosaurs and birds. This fossil exhibited avian and dinosaurian features, such as feathers and teeth, bridging the gap between these two groups and supporting the theory of evolutionary transition.

125. Microraptors had feathers on all four limbs, enabling them to glide and possibly achieve powered flight. This small dinosaur represents an early stage of avian evolution, showcasing the complex adaptations leading to the development of flight in birds.

126. Fossilized dinosaur footprints, known as ichnites, offer valuable insights into dinosaur behavior. These tracks reveal information about their gait, speed, and social interactions, helping paleontologists reconstruct these ancient creatures' daily lives and movements.

As we bid farewell to the mighty dinosaurs and the ancient world they inhabited, our journey through time continues. Dinosaurs, with their immense size and fascinating features, have given us a glimpse into a world long gone. Now, we shift our focus to a different kind of history, one that brings us closer to human times. The story of our planet doesn't end with the extinction of the dinosaurs; it's just the beginning of another exciting chapter filled with human ingenuity, strange customs, and remarkable achievements.

Imagine the Earth evolving over millions of years, transforming from a dinosaur-dominated land into a world shaped by human hands. Our ancestors, much like the dinosaurs, left behind traces of their lives, but instead of fossils, they left artifacts, writings, and traditions. These remnants offer us a window into their daily lives, their beliefs, and the sometimes bizarre practices they followed. From the dawn of civilization to the medieval era and beyond, humans have continuously shaped and reshaped their environment, often in ways that seem peculiar to us today.

Transitioning from the ancient creatures of the prehistoric era to the peculiar practices of our human ancestors allows us to appreciate the continuum of life on Earth. Each era, whether dominated by towering dinosaurs or inventive humans, has its own unique charm and significance. As we move forward, we will uncover the strange and surprising aspects of human history, learning about the odd customs and inventive solutions our ancestors came up with. Get ready to step into a time machine and explore the intriguing and sometimes gross world of historical humans, bridging the gap between the age of dinosaurs and the rich tapestry of human history.

Awesome History

Hey there, young historians and curious minds! Get ready to embark on a fascinating journey through time, venturing far beyond the days of your parents and grandparents. We're diving deep into the pages of history to uncover the strange, surprising, and sometimes downright gross things our ancestors did. Prepare to be amazed and entertained as we explore the wild and wacky world of the past!

Imagine living in a time when people believed in all sorts of weird and beautiful things. From bizarre medical practices to unusual fashion trends, history is filled with stories that will make you gasp, laugh, and maybe even cringe a little. As we travel through different eras, you'll discover how people from ancient civilizations to the medieval ages lived their daily lives, faced challenges, and celebrated their successes.

Did you know that ancient Egyptians used to wear makeup made from crushed beetles and lead? Or did people in the Middle Ages think that bathing too often was bad for your health? These are just a few of the quirky facts we'll uncover as we delve into history's strange side. You'll learn about unusual inventions, peculiar customs, and the odd ways our ancestors tried to understand the world around them.

One of the most exciting parts of studying history is that it helps us see how far we've come and appreciate our progress. While some of the things our ancestors did might seem strange to us today, they also show us the creativity and resourcefulness of people throughout the ages. By exploring these historical oddities, we can better understand how human knowledge and culture have evolved over time.

So, wear your time-traveling hats and prepare for an adventure through the ages! From ancient rituals and medieval medicine to oddball inventions and peculiar pastimes, we're about to uncover the weird and wonderful world of our ancestors. Get ready to be surprised, amazed, and maybe even a little grossed out as we journey through history together!

127. The Great Pyramid of Giza in Egypt, one of the oldest and largest pyramids in the world, was constructed over 4,500 years ago. This monumental structure was built for Pharaoh Khufu and remains a testament to the architectural prowess and engineering skills of ancient Egyptian civilization. Standing at approximately 146 meters (481 feet) originally, it was the tallest man-made structure in the world for over 3,800 years.

128. The Library of Alexandria in Egypt, established in the 3rd century BCE, was one of the ancient world's largest and most significant libraries. It housed thousands of scrolls containing knowledge and stories from various cultures and civilizations. The library aimed to collect all the world's knowledge and became a center of learning and scholarship, attracting scholars from different parts of the world.

129. King Hammurabi of Babylon created one of the earliest and most comprehensive sets of laws in ancient history, known as the Code of Hammurabi. Inscribed on a large stone stele around 1754 BCE, these laws provided a legal framework for justice, covering aspects such as trade, property, family, and crime. The Code of Hammurabi is a significant milestone in the development of legal systems.

130. The ancient Romans engineered impressive aqueducts to transport water from distant sources into cities and towns. These structures, resembling long bridges, were built with a slight gradient to ensure a steady water flow over long distances. The aqueducts supplied fresh water for drinking, bathing, and irrigation, demonstrating Roman ingenuity in public utilities and urban planning.

131. The Indus Valley Civilization flourished around 2500 BCE in what is now Pakistan and northwest India and is renowned for its advanced urban planning. The civilization's cities featured straight streets in a grid pattern, brick houses with complex drainage systems, and large public baths. This high level of sophistication indicates a well-organized and technologically advanced society.

132. The Rosetta Stone, discovered in 1799, is an ancient artifact crucial in deciphering Egyptian hieroglyphs. The stone, dating back to 196 BCE, has the same text inscribed in three scripts: Greek, Demotic, and hieroglyphic. This trilingual inscription allowed scholars, particularly Jean-François Champollion, to unlock the secrets of ancient Egyptian writing, revolutionizing our understanding of Egypt's history and culture.

33

133. According to ancient legends, King Nebuchadnezzar II built the Hanging Gardens of Babylon in the 6th century BCE for his queen, Amytis. These gardens were considered a marvel of engineering, with terraces filled with trees, flowers, and plants, creating the illusion of gardens suspended in the air. Although their existence remains a topic of debate, the Hanging Gardens are considered one of the Seven Wonders of the Ancient World.

134. The magnificent Parthenon, a temple dedicated to the goddess Athena, was constructed on the Acropolis of Athens in the 5th century BCE. This architectural masterpiece epitomizes ancient Greek art and engineering, featuring Doric columns and intricate sculptures. It symbolizes ancient Athens's cultural and political achievements during its Golden Age.

135. The Epic of Gilgamesh, written around 2100 BCE, is one of the oldest known stories in the world. This epic poem from ancient Mesopotamia recounts the adventures of Gilgamesh, the king of Uruk, as he seeks immortality and an understanding of human existence. The narrative explores themes of friendship, heroism, and the human condition, offering valuable insights into early literary traditions.

136. The Silk Road was an extensive network of trade routes connecting China to Europe, facilitating the exchange of goods, ideas, and cultures for over a millennium. Beginning around the 2nd century BCE, merchants traveled along these routes to trade silk, spices, precious metals, and other valuable commodities. The Silk Road was crucial in East and West cultural and economic interactions.

137. The Declaration of Independence, signed on July 4, 1776, marked the American colonies' formal separation from British rule. This historic document, drafted by Thomas Jefferson, articulated the colonies' grievances against King George III and their right to self-governance. The Declaration laid the foundation for the United States of America and its principles of liberty and democracy.

138. According to legend, Betsy Ross sewed the first American flag in 1776, featuring 13 stars and 13 stripes representing the original 13 colonies. This iconic design has evolved but remains a powerful symbol of American identity and unity. Ross's contribution is celebrated in American folklore, although historical evidence of her precise role is limited.

139. The Statue of Liberty, a gift from France to the United States, was dedicated on October 28, 1886. Designed by Frédéric Auguste Bartholdi and engineered by Gustave Eiffel, it symbolizes freedom, democracy, and the enduring friendship between the two nations. Standing on Liberty Island in New York Harbor has become an emblem of hope and a welcoming sight for immigrants arriving in America.

140. In 1903, Orville and Wilbur Wright achieved the first powered, controlled flight with their airplane, the Wright Flyer, in Kitty Hawk, North Carolina. This groundbreaking event marked the beginning of the aviation era, transforming transportation and making the world more interconnected. The Wright brothers' innovation paved the way for the development of modern aircraft and aerospace technology.

141. In 1867, the United States purchased Alaska from Russia for $7.2 million, a deal negotiated by Secretary of State William H. Seward. Initially ridiculed as "Seward's Folly," the acquisition proved valuable due to Alaska's abundant natural resources, including gold, oil, and fish. The purchase expanded U.S. territory and had significant economic and strategic implications.

142. The Civil Rights Act of 1964 was a landmark piece of legislation in the United States that aimed to end segregation and discrimination based on race, color, religion, sex, or national origin. Signed into law by President Lyndon B. Johnson, it represented a significant victory for the Civil Rights Movement and laid the groundwork for further advancements in equality and justice.

143. On July 20, 1969, NASA's Apollo 11 mission successfully landed astronauts Neil Armstrong and Buzz Aldrin on the moon. Armstrong's first steps on the lunar surface and his famous words, "That's one small step for man, one giant leap for mankind," marked a historic achievement in space exploration. The moon landing showcased human ingenuity and the potential for future space endeavors.

144. The Great Depression began with the stock market crash in 1929 and led to a severe economic crisis throughout the 1930s. It resulted in widespread unemployment, poverty, and hardship in the United States and globally. The Depression prompted significant changes in monetary policies and government intervention, shaping modern financial systems and social welfare programs.

145. In 1773, the Boston Tea Party became a pivotal event leading to the American Revolution. In protest against the British Tea Act, American colonists disguised as Mohawk Indians boarded British ships and dumped 342 chests of tea into Boston Harbor. This defiance against taxation without representation galvanized colonial resistance and escalated tensions with Britain.

146. Harriet Tubman, a former enslaved woman, became a leading conductor on the Underground Railroad, helping hundreds of enslaved people escape to freedom before and during the Civil War. Her courage, determination, and strategic insight earned her the nickname "Moses," she remains a symbol of resilience and the fight for liberty and justice.

147. Contrary to popular belief, the Great Wall of China is not easily visible from space without aid. Its visibility depends on lighting, weather conditions, and the observer's eyesight. Built over centuries to protect against invasions, the Great Wall stretches over 13,000 miles and is a testament to ancient Chinese engineering and military strategy.

148. During a hunting party, Napoleon Bonaparte's chief of staff arranged a rabbit hunt with tame rabbits. However, instead of

fleeing, the rabbits saw Napoleon and his party as a source of food and swarmed them, resulting in a humorous and chaotic scene. This unexpected turn of events became a quirky anecdote in Napoleon's storied life.

149. The shortest, oldest, and most commonly used word in English is "I." This single-letter pronoun is fundamental to English grammar and has been used for over a thousand years. Its simplicity and frequent use underscore its importance in communication and self-expression.

150. Mark Twain's "Tom Sawyer" is the first novel written on a typewriter. An early adopter of new technologies, Twain produced his manuscript on a Remington typewriter, highlighting the intersection of literary creativity and technological innovation.

151. Before the invention of the eraser, artists, and scribes used bread to remove pencil marks. A piece of crustless bread was gently rubbed on the paper to erase pencil lines without damaging the surface, demonstrating the inventive use of everyday materials in artistic practices.

152. Louis XIV of France, known as the Sun King, is the longest-reigning monarch, ruling for 72 years and 110 days. His reign profoundly shaped French history and culture, with significant developments in art, architecture, and governance, epitomized by the construction of the Palace of Versailles.

153. In ancient Greece, throwing an apple at someone was a symbolic declaration of love. This custom signified an offer of affection and romantic interest, reflecting the cultural importance of symbolism and gestures in expressing emotions in Greek society.

154. The first passenger train service began in 1807 with the Swansea and Mumbles Railway in Wales. This pioneering service marked the beginning of public rail transport, facilitating

the movement of people alongside freight and heralding a new era in transportation.

155. Contrary to popular depictions, Roman gladiators primarily followed a vegetarian diet. They consumed barley, beans, and dried fruit to maintain their energy and physical endurance, highlighting the nutritional strategies of ancient athletes.

156. The oldest known "your mom" joke was discovered on a 3,500-year-old Babylonian tablet. This early example of humor shows that playful banter and witty remarks were appreciated in ancient civilizations, much like they are today.

157. Julius Caesar was once kidnapped by pirates while traveling across the Aegean Sea. During his captivity, Caesar maintained his composure, joked with his captors, and even demanded a higher ransom. After his release, he pursued and captured the pirates, exacting revenge by crucifying them.

158. The world's oldest known teddy bear, created over 110 years ago, was made by Morris Michtom in 1902. Inspired by a cartoon of President Theodore "Teddy" Roosevelt sparing a bear cub, this beloved toy has become an enduring symbol of childhood and comfort.

159. The Leaning Tower of Pisa has been tilting since its construction in the 12th century due to an unstable foundation. Despite numerous efforts to stabilize it, the tilt remains a defining feature, attracting millions of tourists and making it an iconic landmark.

160. Anne Frank's diary, written during the Holocaust, has been translated into over 70 languages. Her poignant and personal account of life in hiding provides valuable insights into the experiences of Jews during World War II and continues to educate and inspire readers worldwide.

161. The Aztecs used cocoa beans as currency, valuing them for their role in making chocolate and as a medium of exchange in trade.

This practice underscores the cultural and economic significance of cocoa in Mesoamerican societies.

162. Queen Victoria survived seven assassination attempts during her 63-year reign, one of the longest in British history. Despite these threats, she remained a resilient and influential monarch, presiding over significant political and social changes.

163. The "S.O.S." distress signal was officially adopted in 1908 due to its simple and easily recognizable Morse code pattern (three dots, three dashes, three dots). It has become a universal call for help, used by ships and aircraft in emergencies worldwide.

164. The Colosseum in Rome could hold up to 80,000 spectators and hosted various public spectacles, including gladiatorial contests, animal hunts, and dramas. This iconic amphitheater remains a symbol of ancient Roman engineering and entertainment.

165. The Black Death, which struck Europe in the 14th century, killed an estimated 25-30 million people. This devastating plague drastically reduced the population and had profound social, economic, and cultural impacts, reshaping European history.

166. Cleopatra and Julius Caesar had a son, Ptolemy XV Philopator Philometor Caesar, commonly known as Caesarion. As the last Pharaoh of Egypt, Caesarion's lineage represented the political and personal alliance between Egypt and Rome.

167. Johannes Gutenberg's invention of the printing press in the mid-15th century revolutionized the spread of information and literacy. This technological breakthrough made books more accessible, leading to the Renaissance and Reformation and profoundly influencing modern society.

168. The Pony Express: The Pony Express operated for only 18 months from 1860 to 1861, yet it became legendary for connecting the eastern United States with California. Riders traveled across rugged terrain to deliver mail quickly, symbolizing the adventurous spirit of the American frontier.

169. Leonardo da Vinci's "Mona Lisa" was stolen from the Louvre in 1911 by Vincenzo Peruggia, an Italian handyman. The painting was missing for two years before being recovered and returned to the museum, enhancing its fame and intrigue.

170. Built by Mughal Emperor Shah Jahan in memory of his wife, Mumtaz Mahal, the Taj Mahal changes color throughout the day. The white marble monument appears pinkish in the morning, milky white in the evening, and golden under the moonlight, reflecting its ethereal beauty and architectural brilliance.

171. Marco Polo's travels to Asia, lasting 24 years from 1271 to 1295, greatly expanded European knowledge of the Far East. His detailed accounts of China, Persia, and other regions fascinated readers and inspired future explorers.

172. The Mayan civilization developed an advanced writing system using hieroglyphs to record their history, rituals, and knowledge. These intricate symbols, inscribed on codices made from bark paper, provide valuable insights into Mayan culture and achievements.

173. The Eiffel Tower, initially intended to be dismantled after 20 years, was saved from demolition in 1909 due to its usefulness as a giant radio antenna. This iconic structure, designed by Gustave Eiffel, remains one of the most recognizable landmarks in the world and a symbol of Paris.

174. The Eiffel Tower can be 15 cm taller during the summer. When a substance heats up, it expands. This principle applies to the iron structure of the Eiffel Tower. During hot summer days, the metal can expand enough to grow the tower by up to 15 centimeters (6 inches). Conversely, the metal contracts in winter, making the tower slightly shorter.

175. The Magna Carta, signed in 1215, is a foundational document of Western legal tradition. This charter limited the king's powers and established certain legal rights, influencing many future legal systems and constitutions, including the United States.

176. Cleopatra lived closer in time to the Moon landing than to the construction of the Great Pyramid of Giza. Cleopatra lived from 69 to 30 BC and was born over 2,000 years after the Great Pyramid was built (around 2560 BC) and only about 2,000 years before the Moon landing in 1969 AD. This fact illustrates the vast span of human history.

As we conclude our exploration of the strange and sometimes gross practices of our ancestors, we find ourselves on the brink of another fascinating journey. The human story is not just about the customs and inventions of people long gone, but also about the ever-changing world they inhabited. The landscape of our planet has played a crucial role in shaping civilizations, influencing cultures, and determining the course of history.

From the rise of ancient civilizations along fertile river valleys to the strategic importance of mountainous regions in medieval times, geography has always been intertwined with human history. The mountains, rivers, and seas that form our planet's surface have directed the flow of migration, trade, and conflict. As we transition into our next chapter, we'll discover how these natural features have not only influenced where people settled but also how they lived, worked, and interacted with each other.

Imagine the great explorers of history setting out to map uncharted territories, driven by a curiosity to understand the world beyond their borders. These adventurers faced treacherous seas, vast deserts, and towering mountains, their discoveries reshaping the known world and opening new paths for trade and cultural exchange. The ever-changing geography of Earth has constantly challenged and inspired humanity, leading to innovations in navigation, agriculture, and architecture.

As we delve into the captivating and ever-changing geography of our planet, we'll see how natural events like volcanic eruptions, earthquakes, and shifting tectonic plates have shaped the world we know today. These dynamic processes have created the landscapes that have been both a source of sustenance and a challenge for human societies. By understanding the powerful forces that continue to mold our planet, we gain a deeper appreciation for the resilience and adaptability of human beings throughout history.

So, as we leave behind the quirky customs and inventive practices of our ancestors, let's embark on a new adventure to explore the wonders of Earth's geography. This next chapter will reveal the intricate connections between the physical world and human history, showing us how the land beneath our feet has always been an integral part of our story. Get ready to discover the captivating and ever-changing geography of our incredible planet!

Fascinating Geography

Hey there, young explorers and curious minds! Get ready to embark on an incredible journey across our planet's diverse and ever-changing geography. Earth is filled with wonders, from fiery underwater volcanoes to continents that are slowly drifting apart and even islands that mysteriously disappear. This chapter will take you on an adventure to discover the captivating forces that shape our world.

Have you ever wondered what lies beneath the ocean's surface? Our planet is home to thousands of underwater volcanoes, some of which are still active today. These fiery mountains erupt with molten lava, creating new landforms and reshaping the ocean floor. It's like a never-ending fireworks show beneath the waves! We'll dive deep to explore these volcanic wonders and learn how they contribute to the dynamic nature of our planet.

But the excitement doesn't stop there. Did you know that continents are constantly moving? That's right! The Earth's crust is made up of huge slabs called tectonic plates that float on molten rock beneath them. These plates are slowly but surely drifting apart, bumping into each other, and sometimes even creating massive earthquakes. We'll uncover the science behind these movements and how they have shaped today's geography.

Imagine living on an island one day and discovering it's gone the next. Throughout history, islands have appeared and disappeared due to natural forces such as volcanic eruptions, erosion, and rising sea levels. These disappearing islands tell us amazing stories about the power of nature and the ever-changing face of our planet. We'll explore some of these mysterious islands and the incredible events that caused them to vanish.

One of the most thrilling parts of studying Earth's geography is understanding how interconnected everything is. The movement of tectonic plates, volcanic eruptions, and shifting landscapes are all part of a grand system that constantly shapes our world. By exploring these phenomena, we gain a deeper appreciation for the dynamic planet we call home. So, grab your maps and compasses, and let's embark on a journey to discover the wonders of Earth's ever-changing geography!

177. The Sahara Desert can reach 136 degrees Fahrenheit (57 degrees Celsius), making it one of the hottest places on Earth. It spans over 9 million square kilometers and covers much of North Africa. Its vast, arid landscape is characterized by dunes, rocky plateaus, and occasional oases that starkly contrast the otherwise harsh environment.

178. Antarctica is the driest, windiest, and coldest continent. Despite being covered in ice, Antarctica receives very little precipitation, making it a cold desert. Winds can reach up to 200 miles per hour, and temperatures can drop to as low as -128.6 degrees Fahrenheit (-89.2 degrees Celsius). These extreme conditions make it one of the most inhospitable places on Earth, yet it remains a crucial area for scientific research.

179. Maine is the only state in the US whose name is just one syllable. This unique distinction sets Maine apart from the other 49 states. Known for its rugged coastline, dense forests, and maritime history, Maine offers a wealth of natural beauty and cultural heritage. Its simplicity in name reflects the straightforward and unpretentious nature of its landscapes and people.

180. Canada has more lakes than the rest of the world combined. With over 2 million lakes, Canada boasts diverse freshwater ecosystems. These lakes play a crucial role in the country's environment, providing habitats for countless species of plants and animals. The abundance of lakes also supports various recreational activities, such as boating, fishing, and swimming, making Canada a paradise for outdoor enthusiasts.

181. More than 2,000 languages are spoken in Africa. This linguistic diversity reflects the continent's rich cultural heritage and history. Each language represents a unique identity and way of life, contributing to the vibrant tapestry of African societies. Efforts to preserve and promote these languages are essential for maintaining the continent's cultural diversity in the face of globalization and modernization.

182. Alaska has the highest percentage of people who walk to work. The state's rugged terrain and often harsh weather conditions make walking a practical and popular mode of transportation for many residents. Additionally, the sense of community and the desire to reduce environmental impact contributes to the high walking rates, fostering a healthier and more connected lifestyle.

183. The Amazon rainforest produces more than 20% of the world's oxygen. Often referred to as the "lungs of the Earth," the Amazon's dense vegetation plays a critical role in global climate regulation and carbon sequestration. The rainforest's vast biodiversity supports countless species, many of which are yet to be discovered, highlighting the importance of conservation efforts to protect this vital ecosystem.

184. The Pacific Ocean covers more area than all the landmasses on Earth combined. With a surface area of over 63 million square miles, the Pacific Ocean is the largest and deepest ocean on the planet. It plays a crucial role in regulating the Earth's climate, supporting marine biodiversity, and facilitating global trade. Its vast expanse is home to diverse ecosystems, from coral reefs to deep-sea trenches, each contributing to the ocean's complexity and importance.

185. Russia has 11 time zones. This immense country spans Europe and Asia, covering various climates, landscapes, and cultures. Its vastness means that different regions can experience vastly different weather and daylight conditions simultaneously, making it a unique and diverse nation.

186. The Nile River is the longest in the world, measuring 6,650 km (4,130 miles) long. Flowing through 11 countries in northeastern Africa, the Nile has been a lifeline for civilizations for thousands of years. Its waters support agriculture, transportation, and daily life for millions of people. The river's historical significance and modern importance make it one of the most iconic waterways on Earth.

187. The northernmost town in the world is Longyearbyen in Svalbard, Norway, where the sun doesn't set for four months during summer

188. Japan consists of over 6,800 islands. The four largest islands— Honshu, Hokkaido, Kyushu, and Shikoku—comprise most of the country's land area and population. The remaining smaller islands contribute to Japan's rich biodiversity, cultural heritage,

and strategic importance. Each island has unique characteristics, from bustling cities to tranquil rural landscapes.

189. The Dead Sea is so salty that swimmers can float on its surface. With a salinity of around 34%, the Dead Sea is one of the saltiest bodies of water in the world. This high salt concentration creates buoyancy, allowing people to float effortlessly. The mineral-rich waters are also believed to have therapeutic properties, attracting visitors seeking health benefits and relaxation.

190. Australia is the only continent without an active volcano. While it has a history of volcanic activity, the continent's volcanoes are currently dormant. Australia's geological stability is due to its location on the relatively inactive Indo-Australian tectonic plate. This lack of volcanic activity contrasts with the Pacific Ring of Fire, where tectonic activity is frequent and intense.

191. Monaco is smaller than Central Park in New York City. Covering just 2.02 square kilometers, Monaco is the second smallest country in the world after Vatican City. Despite its small size, Monaco is known for its wealth, luxury, and glamorous events, such as the Monaco Grand Prix and the annual yacht show. The country's compact area is densely populated and highly developed.

192. Algeria is Africa's largest country by land area. Its diverse landscape spans nearly 2.4 million square kilometers, including part of the Sahara Desert, mountain ranges, and a Mediterranean coastline. The country's rich history, cultural heritage, and natural resources make it a significant regional player.

193. Mount Everest grows about 4 millimeters higher every year. The Himalayan mountain range, including Mount Everest, continues to rise due to the tectonic collision between the Indian and Eurasian plates. This ongoing geological activity heightens the world's tallest peak and the dynamic and ever-changing nature of Earth's surface.

194. The Maldives has the lowest highest point of any country. The highest natural point in the Maldives is only 2.4 meters (7 feet 10 inches) above sea level. This low elevation makes the island nation particularly vulnerable to rising sea levels caused by climate change. The Maldives' stunning coral atolls and marine biodiversity attract tourists worldwide, but the threat of submersion looms large.

195. Singapore is the only island city-state in the world. Comprising one main island and 62 smaller islets, Singapore is a global financial hub known for its clean, modern infrastructure and diverse population. Despite its small geographic size, the city-state's strategic location, efficient governance, and vibrant economy have transformed it into a significant international player.

196. Vatican City is the smallest country in the world. Encompassing just 44 hectares (110 acres), Vatican City is an independent city-state in Rome, Italy. As the spiritual and administrative center of the Roman Catholic Church, it houses significant religious and cultural landmarks, including St. Peter's Basilica and the Vatican Museums.

197. Argentina's name comes from the Latin word for silver, 'argentum.' Early European explorers believed the region was rich in silver, hence the name. Although large silver deposits were never found, Argentina's name reflects the initial hopes and legends that drew explorers to South America. Argentina is known for its diverse landscapes, vibrant culture, and significant contributions to art, music, and cuisine.

198. Bhutan is the only country in the world that measures its progress by Gross National Happiness. Instead of focusing solely on economic growth, Bhutan prioritizes the well-being and happiness of its citizens. This unique approach encompasses sustainable development, cultural preservation, environmental conservation, and good governance, making Bhutan a pioneer in holistic development.

199. Istanbul, Turkey, is the only city on two continents. Straddling the Bosphorus Strait, it connects Europe and Asia. For centuries, this unique position has been a critical crossroads of civilizations, trade, and culture. The city's rich history, blending of Eastern and Western influences, and vibrant modern life make it one of the world's most fascinating urban centers.

200. Greenland is the world's largest island. Despite being covered in ice, Greenland spans over 2.1 million square kilometers. Towering glaciers, deep fjords, and sparse vegetation characterize its vast, remote landscape. The island's indigenous Inuit culture and stunning natural beauty make it a fascinating destination for adventurous travelers and researchers.

201. There's a spot in the Pacific Ocean called the 'Point Nemo,' the farthest place from any land, making it the most remote point on Earth.

202. Canada has the second-largest land area globally, spanning six time zones and showcasing diverse climates and landscapes

203. Tbig he Nile River is the longest in the world, measuring 6,650 km (4,130 miles) long. Flowing through 11 countries in northeastern Africa, the Nile has been a lifeline for civilizations for thousands of years. Its waters support agriculture, transportation, and daily life for millions of people. The river's historical significance and modern importance make it one of the most iconic waterways on Earth.

204. There is a town in Norway called Hell, and it freezes over every winter. Located in central Norway, Hell is a small village that experiences freezing temperatures during winter. The name has attracted tourists and curiosity seekers, especially those interested in the novelty of visiting "Hell" and seeing it freeze over.

205. The Philippines consists of over 7,000 islands, with only about 2,000 inhabited, offering diverse ecosystems and cultures

206. Lake Natron in Tanzania is so alkaline that it can calcify animals that come into contact with it, creating natural mummies.

207. Iceland has over 130 active and inactive volcanoes, earning it the nickname 'Land of Fire and Ice'".

208. Monaco is smaller than Central Park in New York City. At just 2.02 square kilometers, it is the second smallest country in the world after Vatican City. Despite its small size, Monaco is known for its wealth, luxury, and glamorous events, such as the Monaco Grand Prix and the annual yacht show. The country's compact area is densely populated and highly developed.

209. Sudan, once the largest country in Africa, was divided in 2011 to form South Sudan, reshaping its geographical significance.

210. Mount Everest grows about 4 millimeters higher every year. The Himalayan mountain range, including Mount Everest, continues to rise due to the tectonic collision between the Indian and Eurasian plates. This ongoing geological activity heightens the world's tallest peak and contributes to Earth's surface's dynamic and ever-changing nature.

211. The Maldives has the lowest highest point of any country. The highest natural point in the Maldives is only 2.4 meters (7 feet 10 inches) above sea level. This low elevation makes the island nation particularly vulnerable to rising sea levels caused by climate change. The Maldives' stunning coral atolls and marine biodiversity attract tourists worldwide, but the threat of submersion looms large.

212. Singapore is the only island city-state in the world. Comprising one main island and 62 smaller islets, Singapore is a global financial hub known for its clean, modern infrastructure and diverse population. Despite its small geographic size, the city-state's strategic location, efficient governance, and vibrant economy have transformed it into a significant international player.

213. The Principality of Sealand, located on a former WWII sea fort, is one of the smallest self-proclaimed nations, covering just 0.004 square kilometers.

214. Chile is named after the indigenous word 'chilli,' which means 'where the land ends,' referencing its long, narrow shape..

215. New Zealand is known for prioritizing the well-being of its citizens, ranking consistently high in the World Happiness Report due to its focus on health, safety, and environmental sustainability.

216. Panama City is the only capital city in the world where you can see both the Pacific Ocean and the Atlantic Ocean from the same location.

217. Africa's largest country by land area is Algeria, which spans nearly 2.4 million square kilometers. This vast nation features a diverse landscape, from the sprawling Sahara Desert in the south to the Mediterranean coastline in the north. Algeria's rich cultural heritage and natural beauty make it a unique and significant country on the African continent.

218. Norway is home to Hell, a small town that experiences freezing temperatures every winter. Located in central Norway, Hell becomes a popular point of interest due to its unusual name and the ironic phrase "when Hell freezes over," which happens each winter as temperatures drop below freezing.

219. The Amazon River, renowned for its sheer size and volume, is the second-longest river in the world, spanning about 4,345 miles (7,062 kilometers). This mighty river discharges more water than any other river, supporting an incredibly diverse ecosystem that includes numerous species of fish, plants, and animals unique to the Amazon rainforest.

220. The Atacama Desert in Chile is recognized as the driest place on Earth. Some areas have never recorded rainfall, creating an extremely arid environment. Despite its harsh conditions, the

Atacama is home to unique flora and fauna adapted to survive with minimal water.

221. The Mariana Trench, located in the western Pacific Ocean, is the deepest in the world's oceans. It reaches a maximum known depth of about 36,070 feet (10,994 meters). Due to its extreme depths and unique life forms, this underwater trench is a subject of scientific exploration and fascination.

222. Lake Baikal in Russia is the world's deepest and oldest freshwater lake. With a depth of over 5,387 feet (1,642 meters) and an age of about 25 million years, Baikal is a geological wonder and a biodiversity hotspot hosting numerous endemic species.

223. The Great Barrier Reef in Australia is the world's most extensive coral reef system, spanning over 2,300 kilometers. This natural wonder is home to thousands of marine species, including fish, corals, and other aquatic life, making it one of the planet's most diverse and complex ecosystems.

224. Tonga, a Pacific island nation located just west of the International Date Line, is the first country to see the sunrise daily. This unique geographic position makes Tonga a fascinating place for travelers and a symbol of new beginnings as it greets the first light of the day before any other country.

As we wrap up our journey through the captivating and ever-changing geography of our planet, it's clear that Earth's dynamic nature is full of wonders that have shaped both the land and human history. But our exploration of the natural world doesn't end here. Next, we'll dive into a different kind of adventure, one that takes us into the heart of the scientific world, where incredible experiments and bizarre reactions await.

Just as the forces of nature sculpt mountains and create islands, the principles of science help us understand how and why these phenomena occur. Moving from the vast landscapes of our planet to the microscopic and atomic levels of scientific inquiry, we'll discover the fascinating interactions that govern our world. By exploring the wonders of science, we'll see how curiosity and experimentation can reveal the secrets of the universe, from the explosive reactions of certain metals to the intriguing properties of materials that defy our expectations.

Our transition from geography to science is a journey from the big picture to the intricate details that make up everything around us. By understanding both the grand and the minuscule, we gain a deeper appreciation for the complexity and beauty of the world we live in. So, as we leave behind the wonders of Earth's landscapes, let's jump into the exciting realm of scientific discovery and prepare to be amazed by the incredible experiments and bizarre reactions that await us.

Incredible Science

Hey there, young explorers and budding scientists! Get ready to jump into a world filled with incredible experiments and bizarre reactions. Science is all around us, and it's more amazing than you can imagine. From exploding metals to substances that can freeze and melt at the same time, we are about to uncover some of the coolest and most surprising phenomena that science has to offer.

Imagine watching a simple piece of metal suddenly burst into flames or explode. It might sound like something out of a movie, but it's real science! Metals like sodium and potassium can react explosively when they come into contact with water. These spectacular reactions happen because of the unique properties of these metals, and they give us a glimpse into the powerful forces at work in the natural world. We'll dive into these explosive experiments and learn what makes them so astonishing.

Have you ever heard of a substance that can be both solid and liquid at the same time? It sounds impossible, but it's true! Some materials, like gallium, can melt in your hand but still hold their shape in a cool room. There are also fascinating materials called non-Newtonian fluids that can act like a solid when you hit them but flow like a liquid when you gently touch them. These strange and wonderful substances challenge our understanding of what it means to be solid or liquid, and we'll explore the science behind these amazing reactions.

Science isn't just about big explosions and weird substances, though. It's also about understanding the everyday phenomena that happen all around us. Why does ice float on water? How does a microwave heat your food? By asking questions and conducting experiments, we can uncover the secrets behind these ordinary occurrences. We'll learn how to think like scientists, using curiosity and creativity to explore the world and discover its hidden wonders.

One of the best parts of science is that it's always changing and growing. New discoveries are made every day, leading to even more questions and exciting possibilities. As we explore the incredible experiments and bizarre reactions in this chapter, you'll see how science is a never-ending adventure. There's always something new to learn and explore, and who knows? Maybe one day, you'll be the one making the next big scientific breakthrough!

So, grab your lab coats and safety goggles, and get ready for a thrilling journey into the world of science. From exploding metals to melting solids, we'll uncover the wonders of chemistry, physics, and more. Get ready to be amazed by the incredible experiments and bizarre reactions that make science so exciting!

225. Water can boil and freeze simultaneously. This phenomenon, known as the triple point, occurs at a specific combination of temperature and pressure. For water, the triple point is 0.01°C (32.018°F) at a pressure of 611.657 pascals. At this precise point, water can exist simultaneously as a solid (ice), a liquid, and a gas (vapor), creating a unique and fascinating state of equilibrium.

226. Bananas are radioactive. Bananas contain potassium-40, a naturally occurring radioactive isotope. While the radiation levels are deficient and harmless to humans, it is interesting to note that consuming a large quantity of bananas would expose you to a small amount of radiation. This radioactive property of bananas is often used as a reference point for discussing radiation levels in various contexts.

227. The average person produces about one pound of poo per day, which totals around 360 pounds a year. This significant amount underscores the efficiency and constancy of the human digestive system.

228. Lightning can heat the air to around 30,000 degrees Celsius, about five times hotter than the sun's surface. The extreme heat causes the surrounding air to rapidly expand and contract, creating the shockwave we heard as thunder. Despite its ferocity, the average lightning bolt is relatively short-lived, lasting only a few microseconds.

229. Sound travels about four times faster in water than in air. This increased speed is due to the denser water medium, which allows sound waves to propagate more efficiently. Marine animals like whales and dolphins rely on this phenomenon for underwater communication, navigation, and hunting.

230. Some metals are so reactive that they explode in contact with water. Metals like potassium, sodium, and cesium react violently with water, producing heat, hydrogen gas, and a corresponding explosion. These reactions are often used in educational demonstrations to illustrate the principles of chemical reactivity and the properties of alkali metals.

231. Bamboo can grow up to 91 cm in a day. Certain species of bamboo are among the fastest-growing plants on Earth. Their rapid growth rate is due to their unique structure and efficient use of nutrients. Bamboo is a versatile and sustainable resource used in construction, furniture, and even as a food source.

232. The planet Mars has the largest dust storms in the solar system. These storms can cover the entire planet and last for months, significantly impacting surface conditions. The dust is fine and can be carried high into the atmosphere, creating a dramatic and challenging environment for future human exploration.

233. The speed of light in a vacuum is about 299,792 kilometers per second. This constant speed is fundamental to physics and underpins many scientific theories and principles. It is the fastest speed at which information or matter can travel, forming the basis for our understanding of space and time.

234. There is a special measure for poos called a Bristol Stool Chart, which classifies stool into seven types, with Type 4 considered the healthiest. Consistency and shape can reflect digestive health and hydration levels.

235. It is physically impossible for pigs to look up into the sky. The structure of a pig's neck muscles and spine makes it difficult for them to lift their heads high enough to look directly upwards. Despite this limitation, pigs are highly intelligent animals with a keen sense of smell and the ability to learn and remember complex tasks.

236. Astronauts grow taller in space. Without the constant pull of Earth's gravity, the spine can expand, allowing astronauts to grow by up to 2 inches during their time in space. This temporary increase in height is reversed upon returning to Earth as gravity compresses the spine to its usual length.

237. If you could fold a piece of paper 42 times, it would reach the moon. While it may seem impossible, the exponential growth in thickness with each fold means that a paper folded 42 times

would be thick enough to span approximately 384,400 kilometers (238,855 miles) to the moon. In reality, physical limitations prevent folding paper more than about seven times.

238. Unlike most substances, water expands when it freezes. This unusual property is due to the hydrogen bonding between water molecules, which are arranged in a crystalline structure that takes up more space than in liquid form. This is why ice is less dense than liquid water and floats on its surface, a characteristic vital for aquatic life during cold seasons.

239. Light from the Sun takes about 8 minutes and 20 seconds to reach Earth, traveling at an astonishing speed of approximately 299,792 kilometers per second (186,282 miles per second). This rapid journey across 149.6 million kilometers (93 million miles) highlights the immense speed of light and the vast distances in our solar system.

240. Earth is approximately 4.5 billion years old, a figure determined by dating the oldest rocks and meteorites. This immense age reflects our planet's long and complex history, from its formation from cosmic dust to the development of life and the evolution of its geological features.

241. The speed of a blow-off as it exits the body is approximately 10 feet per second or about 7 miles per hour.

242. Only about 1% of the sunlight that hits a plant is used in photosynthesis to produce organic compounds. This efficiency is relatively low, considering the vast amount of solar energy plants receive. Nonetheless, photosynthesis is critical for life on Earth, converting solar energy into chemical energy and producing oxygen.

243. In quantum mechanics, particles like electrons can exist simultaneously in multiple states or locations until they are measured or observed. This phenomenon, known as quantum superposition, defies classical intuition and underlies many of quantum systems' strange and counterintuitive behaviors.

244. More than 80% of the ocean remains unexplored and unmapped, making it one of the least understood parts of our planet. This vast, mysterious frontier harbors countless undiscovered species and geological features, highlighting the importance and potential of oceanographic research.

245. Saturn is the only planet in our solar system that is less dense than water. If a body of water were large enough, Saturn would float on it. This low density is due to Saturn's composition, primarily hydrogen and helium, which are much lighter than the materials that make up Earth.

246. The Hubble Space Telescope's Deep Field images revealed thousands of galaxies in a tiny patch of sky, providing a glimpse into the vastness of the universe. These images show that the universe is filled with galaxies, each containing billions of stars, demonstrating the immense scale and complexity of the cosmos.

247. The universe has been expanding since the Big Bang, and this expansion is accelerating due to a mysterious force known as dark energy. This discovery has profound implications for our understanding of the cosmos, suggesting that the universe will expand indefinitely.

248. Black holes are regions in space where gravity is so strong that not even light can escape them. They are formed when massive stars collapse under their own gravity, creating a singularity with infinite density and zero volume. Black holes challenge our understanding of physics, particularly the nature of space and time.

249. The Earth's inner core is as hot as the Sun's surface, with temperatures reaching up to 5,700 degrees Celsius (10,292 degrees Fahrenheit). This intense heat is generated by the decay of radioactive elements and the residual heat from the planet's formation, playing a crucial role in driving geological processes.

250. The Earth's magnetic field is generated by the movement of molten iron in its outer core. This magnetic field protects the

planet from the solar wind and cosmic radiation, which would otherwise strip away the atmosphere and harm living organisms. It also causes phenomena like the auroras near the poles.

251. The Earth's crust is divided into several plates that float on the semi-fluid mantle. Their movement causes earthquakes, volcanic activity, and the formation of mountains. Plate tectonics is a fundamental process that shapes the Earth's surface and drives the geological cycle.

252. The ozone layer in the Earth's stratosphere absorbs most of the Sun's harmful ultraviolet radiation, protecting living organisms from its damaging effects. This layer is crucial for maintaining life on Earth, and its depletion due to human activities has raised significant environmental concerns.

253. Nuclear fusion converts hydrogen into helium in stars, including the Sun, releasing enormous amounts of energy. This process powers the stars and provides light and heat to surrounding planets, making it fundamental to life's existence and the universe's dynamics.

254. Neutron stars are incredibly dense. A single teaspoon of neutron star material would weigh about 6 billion tons on Earth. This extreme density is due to the collapse of massive stars, compressing matter to such an extent that protons and electrons combine to form neutrons.

255. Venus rotates backward compared to most planets in the solar system. This retrograde rotation means the Sun rises in the west and sets in the east on Venus, making its day-night cycle unique among the planets.

256. The human body contains enough carbon to make 9,000 pencils. Carbon is one of the most abundant elements in the human body, making up about 18% of our mass and playing a crucial role in our biochemical processes.

257. An adult human comprises approximately seven octillion atoms. This staggering number highlights the complexity and intricacy of the human body at the atomic level, reflecting the vast number of interactions and processes occurring within us.

258. The Andromeda Galaxy is on a collision course with the Milky Way. In about 4 billion years, our galaxy will collide with Andromeda, creating a new galaxy. This event will reshape our cosmic neighborhood but is unlikely to impact individual stars or planetary systems significantly.

259. A day on Mercury lasts longer than a year on Mercury. Mercury takes about 59 Earth days to complete one rotation, but it orbits the Sun in just 88 Earth days. This means that its day-night cycle is longer than its orbital period, creating unique conditions on its surface.

260. The largest volcano in the solar system is Olympus Mons on Mars. It stands about 13.6 miles (22 kilometers) high, nearly three times the height of Mount Everest, and its base is roughly the size of the state of Arizona. Olympus Mons's size and structure offer insights into volcanic activity on Mars.

261. The Earth's atmosphere is mostly nitrogen, comprising about 78%, with oxygen making up about 21%. This composition is crucial for supporting life, as nitrogen is essential for biological processes, and oxygen is necessary for respiration.

262. Hot water can freeze faster than cold water, a counterintuitive phenomenon known as the Mpemba effect. Although its exact causes are still debated, it is thought to involve factors such as evaporation, convection currents, and the behavior of hydrogen bonds in water.

263. There are more stars in the universe than grains of sand on all the Earth's beaches. Estimates suggest around one septillion stars (1 followed by 24 zeros), illustrating the vastness and richness of the cosmos beyond our comprehension.

264. The coldest temperature ever recorded on Earth is -128.6°F (-89.2°C). This record was set at the Soviet Union's Vostok Station in Antarctica on July 21, 1983, highlighting the extreme conditions that can occur on our planet.

265. Water is the only substance that exists naturally on Earth in all three states: solid, liquid, and gas. This versatility is due to its unique molecular structure and hydrogen bonding, which are essential for supporting life and various geological processes.

266. The sound of a blue whale can reach 188 decibels, louder than a jet engine. These sounds can be heard hundreds of miles underwater, demonstrating the blue whale's immense vocal power and ability to communicate across vast ocean distances.

267. A bolt of lightning contains enough energy to toast 100,000 slices of bread. Lightning bolts can carry up to one billion volts of electricity, with a current of up to 200,000 amperes, causing air temperatures to soar to 30,000 degrees Celsius (54,000 degrees Fahrenheit).

268. The Sun accounts for about 99.86% of the solar system's total mass. Its immense gravitational pull governs the orbits of all the planets and other objects, making it the dominant force in our solar system.

269. The highest recorded temperature on Earth is 134°F (56.7°C), recorded in Death Valley, California, on July 10, 1913. This demonstrates the extreme heat that can occur in Earth's deserts.

270. A comet's tail always points away from the Sun, regardless of the comet's direction of travel. This is due to the solar wind, which pushes dust and gas away from the comet's nucleus, forming the characteristic tail seen from Earth.

271. Diamonds rain on Saturn and Jupiter due to the high pressures and temperatures in their atmospheres. These extreme conditions can compress carbon into diamonds, creating a fascinating and exotic form of precipitation.

272. Humans share 60% of their DNA with bananas, a surprising fact underscoring the shared genetic heritage among all living organisms. This genetic similarity highlights the common evolutionary origins of life on Earth.

273. The human brain generates enough electricity to power a small light bulb. Operating on about 20 watts of power, the brain's electrical activity reflects its efficiency and the complexity of neural processes.

274. On average, a person blows off around 14 times a day. This is a normal part of the digestive process and indicates that your digestive system is working properly

275. A lightning bolt is five times hotter than the Sun's surface. Lightning can reach around 30,000 degrees Celsius (54,000 degrees Fahrenheit), far exceeding the Sun's surface temperature of about 5,500 degrees Celsius (9,932 degrees Fahrenheit).

276. The Pacific Ocean is shrinking due to plate tectonics, gradually becoming smaller while the Atlantic Ocean expands. This process is driven by the movement of Earth's tectonic plates, which have reshaped the planet's surface over millions of years.

277. The average human body temperature is not exactly 98.6°F; it varies among individuals and can range from about 97°F to 99°F. This variability reflects individual differences in metabolism, health, and environmental conditions.

278. Humans and giraffes have the same number of neck vertebrae—seven—despite the difference in neck length.

As we leave behind the exciting world of scientific experiments and bizarre reactions, we realize that the quest for knowledge doesn't stop at the boundaries of our planet. Just as we have been amazed by the incredible phenomena happening right here on Earth, there's an even greater expanse waiting to be explored above us. The mysteries of the universe beckon, inviting us to look up at the stars and wonder about the vast cosmos beyond our reach.

Transitioning from the wonders of science that explain our immediate surroundings, we now turn our gaze to the night sky, where countless celestial bodies and cosmic events unfold. The principles we learned about reactions and matter on Earth also apply to the farthest reaches of space, helping us understand the stars, planets, and galaxies that populate our universe. Get ready to embark on a cosmic adventure, discovering the incredible objects zooming past our planet and the enormous celestial wonders that await us in the vast expanse of space.

500 Amazing Facts for Kids

Review Request Page

"Imagination is more important than knowledge. For knowledge is limited, whereas imagination embraces the entire world, stimulating progress, giving birth to evolution." - Albert Einstein undefined

Hey there, future genius! Have you ever wondered why the sky is blue, how fast a cheetah can run, or what it was like when dinosaurs ruled the Earth? This book is your ticket to a world of mind-blowing facts about everything from the mysteries of space to the wonders of the animal kingdom. It's like having a treasure chest packed with the coolest facts just waiting for you to discover!

People who give without expectation live longer, and happier lives . So if we've got a shot at that during our time together, darn it, I'm gonna try.

To make that happen, I have a question for you...

Would you help someone you've never met, even if you never got credit for it?

Who is this person you ask? They are like you. Or, at least, like you used to be. Curious, eager to learn, and hungry for knowledge, but not sure where to find it.

Our mission is to make learning fun and exciting for everyone. Everything I do stems from that mission, and the only way for me to accomplish that mission is by reaching......everyone.

This is where you come in. Most people do, in fact, judge a book by its cover (and its reviews). So here's my ask on behalf of a curious kid you've never met:

Please help that curious kid by leaving this book a review.

Your gift costs no money and takes less than 60 seconds to make real, but it can change a fellow reader's life forever. Your review could help…

…one more kid discovers the joy of learning. …one more teacher inspires their students. …one more parent shares a magical moment with their child. ..one more reader embarks on an amazing journey through facts and fun.

To get that 'feel good' feeling and help this person for real, all you have to do is…and it takes less than 60 seconds… leave a review.

Scan the QR code below to leave your review:

If you feel good about helping a faceless reader, you are my kind of person. Welcome to the club. You're one of us.

I'm that much more excited to help you discover the coolest facts faster than you can possibly imagine. You'll love the amazing stories and facts I'm about to share in the coming pages.

Thank you from the bottom of my heart. Now, back to our regularly scheduled program-ming.

Your biggest fan, Ian Pattle

PS - Fun fact: If you provide something of value to another person, it makes you more valuable to them. If you'd like goodwill straight from another reader - and you believe this book will help them - send this book their way.

Mind-Blowing Space

Hey there, young stargazers and future astronauts! Get ready to embark on an out-of-this-world adventure as we look up at the stars and wonder about the vast universe beyond our planet. The night sky is filled with countless mysteries, and we're about to uncover some of the most incredible objects zooming past Earth and the enormous celestial bodies that make up our universe.

Have you ever gazed up at the night sky and felt a sense of wonder? Those twinkling stars, distant planets, and glowing moons are just a tiny glimpse of the vastness that lies beyond our world. Space is a place where the unimaginable becomes reality, and every star has its own story to tell. From our own solar system to the far reaches of the galaxy, we'll explore the wonders that await us in the cosmos.

Imagine giant asteroids hurtling through space, comets with glowing tails streaking across the sky, and meteors lighting up the night as they burn up in our atmosphere. These objects might seem like science fiction, but they are real and awe-inspiring parts of our universe. We'll learn about the fascinating journeys these celestial travelers take and how they sometimes even visit our planet, bringing with them secrets from the distant past.

But the universe is more than just stars and space rocks. Out there, among the endless stretches of space, are massive planets, brilliant nebulae, and enormous galaxies, each with its own unique characteristics and beauty. Did you know that some stars are so big they could fit millions of Earths inside them? Or that there are black holes with gravitational pulls so strong that nothing, not even light, can escape them? These mind-boggling facts are just the beginning of our exploration into the vastness of space.

One of the most exciting aspects of studying the universe is the sense of discovery and adventure it brings. With each new observation, scientists uncover more about how our universe works, how it began, and what lies beyond what we can see. As we learn about the incredible objects and phenomena in space, we'll also see how the study of astronomy helps us understand our own place in the cosmos.

So, grab your telescopes and star charts, and get ready to embark on a cosmic journey. From the smallest meteors to the largest galaxies, we'll uncover the wonders of the universe and marvel at the incredible sights that await us in the night sky. Get ready to be amazed by the vastness and beauty of space as we explore the wonders of the universe together!

279. One million Earths could fit inside the sun, one million times larger than our home planet. The sun's vast size and mass dwarf

those of our home planet. This immense capacity highlights the scale of our solar system's central star, which provides the energy and light necessary for life on Earth. Understanding the sun's enormity helps us appreciate the vastness and complexity of the cosmos.

280. Mercury's year (one lap around the Sun) is about 88 Earth days long. A solar day on Mercury is twice as long as its year, or about 176 Earth days long. This is because of the slow rotation of Mercury around its axis (e.g., when compared to Earth's rotation)

281. Neutron stars are so dense that a sugar-cube-sized amount of material from one would weigh about a billion tons. These remnants of massive stars are incredibly compact, with their mass packed into a tiny volume. The intense gravity and density of neutron stars result in extreme physical conditions, making them some of the most fascinating objects in the universe.

282. The footprints on the Moon will likely stay there for millions of years. Without an atmosphere, the Moon has no wind or water to erode these marks. The footprints left by astronauts during the Apollo missions are preserved in the lunar dust, providing a lasting legacy of humanity's first steps on another celestial body. These imprints serve as a testament to human exploration and achievement.

283. There are more stars in the universe than grains of sand on all the Earth's beaches combined. The observable universe contains an estimated 100 billion galaxies, each with billions of stars. This staggering number underscores the vastness of the cosmos and the potential for countless planetary systems and, possibly, extraterrestrial life. The comparison to grains of sand helps convey the unimaginable scale of the universe.

284. Venus is the hottest planet in our solar system. With surface temperatures reaching up to 900 degrees Fahrenheit (475 degrees Celsius), Venus is hotter than Mercury, even though it is farther from the sun. This extreme heat is due to Venus's thick atmosphere, composed mainly of carbon dioxide, which creates

a runaway greenhouse effect, trapping heat and preventing it from escaping.

285. If you could travel at the speed of light, reaching the nearest star, Proxima Centauri, would take you over four years. Located 4.24 light-years away, Proxima Centauri is the closest known star to our solar system. Traveling at the speed of light, about 299,792 kilometers per second (186,282 miles per second), would still require more than four years to bridge this vast distance, illustrating the immense scale of interstellar space.

286. Mars has the largest volcano in the solar system, Olympus Mons. Standing nearly 13.6 miles (22 kilometers) high, Olympus Mons is almost three times the height of Mount Everest. Its base is about 370 miles (600 kilometers) in diameter, roughly the size of Arizona. This shield volcano's colossal size and gentle slopes make it one of the most striking features on Mars.

287. The Milky Way galaxy is on a collision course with the Andromeda galaxy. In about 4.5 billion years, these two spiral galaxies are expected to merge in a spectacular event. This cosmic collision will reshape both galaxies, creating a new, larger elliptical galaxy. While stars within the galaxies are unlikely to collide due to the vast distances between them, the gravitational interactions will significantly alter their structures.

288. Space is completely silent because there is no atmosphere for sound to travel through. Sound waves require a medium, such as air or water, to propagate. In the vacuum of space, there are no molecules to carry sound, making it a silent environment. This absence of sound contrasts sharply with the bustling activity and noise experienced on Earth.

289. A day on Venus is longer than its year. Venus takes about 243 Earth days to complete one rotation on its axis but only about 225 Earth days to orbit the sun. This unusual rotation pattern means that a single day on Venus (one full rotation) is longer than its year (one complete orbit around the sun), creating a unique and extreme environment.

290. Saturn's moon, Titan, has lakes and rivers of liquid methane and ethane. Titan's thick atmosphere and frigid temperatures allow these hydrocarbons to exist in liquid form, creating features similar to those found on Earth, such as lakes, rivers, and rain. Despite its vastly different chemistry and conditions, these liquid methane and ethane bodies make Titan one of the most Earth-like places in our solar system.

291. The International Space Station travels at a speed of 28,000 kilometers (17,500 miles) per hour. Orbiting Earth approximately every 90 minutes, the ISS covers vast distances at incredible speeds. This rapid orbit allows astronauts aboard the station to witness 16 sunrises and sunsets daily, providing a unique perspective on our planet's rotation and the passage of time.

292. A day on Venus is longer than a year on Venus. Venus rotates very slowly on its axis, taking about 243 Earth days to complete one rotation. However, it orbits the sun much faster, completing a revolution in 225 Earth days. This means that a single day on Venus (one full rotation) is longer than its year (one complete orbit around the sun), creating a unique and extreme environment.

293. A neutron star's gravity is 2 billion times stronger than Earth's. Its intense gravitational pull results from its incredibly dense mass packed into a small volume. This extreme gravity affects everything around the star, warping space-time and creating powerful gravitational fields that can dramatically influence nearby objects.

294. Pluto, now classified as a dwarf planet, was discovered in 1930. Once considered the ninth planet in our solar system, Pluto was reclassified as a dwarf planet by the International Astronomical Union in 2006. This decision was based on the discovery of similar-sized objects in the Kuiper Belt and the need to refine the definition of a planet. Pluto remains an essential and fascinating object in our understanding of the solar system.

295. It rains diamonds on Saturn and Jupiter. The extreme pressure and temperatures in the atmospheres of these gas giants can cause carbon to crystallize into diamonds. This process begins with methane molecules breaking down into carbon atoms, which fall deeper into the atmosphere and compress into diamond crystals. These diamonds may eventually melt into liquid carbon as they descend into the planets' interiors.

296. Jupiter has the shortest day of all the planets, completing one rotation in under 10 hours. Despite its massive size, Jupiter's rapid rotation creates a day less than half the length of an Earth day. This swift spin contributes to the planet's strong magnetic field and the distinctive bands of clouds and storms, including the Great Red Spot, a massive storm system that has persisted for centuries.

297. There could be over 100 billion galaxies in the observable universe. The Hubble Space Telescope and other advanced observatories have revealed the vastness of the cosmos, uncovering countless galaxies, each containing billions of stars. This mind-boggling number underscores the immense scale and complexity of the universe, with numerous opportunities for the formation of planetary systems and, potentially, life.

298. Black holes aren't holes. They are objects with incredibly strong gravity. Black holes are formed when massive stars collapse under their gravity, creating a region of space where the gravitational pull is so strong that not even light can escape. This intense gravity warps space-time and creates a "point of no return" known as the event horizon. Despite their name, black holes are not empty voids but some of the universe's most extreme and dense objects.

299. A year on Neptune lasts 165 Earth years. Neptune, the eighth and farthest planet from the sun, takes about 165 Earth years to complete one orbit. Since its discovery in 1846, Neptune has only completed one full orbit around the sun. The planet's great distance from the sun results in long, cold seasons and a unique

atmospheric composition, including high-speed winds and giant storms.

300. The Hubble Space Telescope, launched in 1990, has made more than 1.5 million observations since then. It has revolutionized our understanding of the universe. Its observations have provided insights into the universe's age, distant galaxies' behavior, exoplanets' existence, and the nature of dark matter and energy. Hubble's contributions to astronomy and our understanding of the cosmos are unparalleled.

301. Uranus rotates on its side, making it unique among the planets. Unlike the other planets, which rotate on an axis perpendicular to their orbital plane, Uranus has an axial tilt of about 98 degrees. This unusual tilt likely resulted from a massive collision early in the planet's history. It caused extreme seasonal variations, with each pole experiencing 42 years of continuous sunlight followed by 42 years of darkness.

302. The largest moon in our solar system is Ganymede, a moon of Jupiter. With a diameter of about 5,268 kilometers (3,273 miles), Ganymede is even larger than Mercury. It has a complex geological history, including ice, rock, and a magnetic field, which is unusual for a moon. Ganymede's unique features and potential subsurface ocean make it a prime candidate for future exploration.

303. Light from the Sun takes about 8 minutes and 20 seconds to reach Earth. Traveling at the speed of light, photons emitted from the sun traverse the 93 million miles (150 million kilometers) of space to reach our planet. This brief travel time underscores the vast distances within our solar system and the incredible speed of light.

304. Uranus rotates on its side, making it unique among the planets. Unlike the other planets, which rotate on an axis perpendicular to their orbital plane, Uranus has an axial tilt of about 98 degrees. This unusual tilt likely resulted from a massive collision early in the planet's history. It caused extreme seasonal variations, with

each pole experiencing 42 years of continuous sunlight followed by 42 years of darkness.

305. There are five known dwarf planets in our solar system: Pluto, Ceres, Haumea, Makemake, and Eris. These small celestial bodies share characteristics with planets and smaller solar system objects. They orbit the sun and have sufficient mass to assume a nearly round shape but have not cleared their orbits of other debris. The study of dwarf planets provides valuable insights into the formation and evolution of our solar system.

306. A day on the moon is about 29.5 Earth days. The moon is tidally locked with Earth, meaning the same side always faces us.

307. The Milky Way is on a collision course with the Andromeda Galaxy. The two galaxies will merge in about 4 billion years, forming a new galaxy.

308. The coldest place in the universe is the Boomerang Nebula, about 5,000 light-years away. This fascinating nebula has a temperature of -458 degrees Fahrenheit (-272 degrees Celsius), just one degree above absolute zero, making it the coldest known natural environment in the cosmos.

309. In 1947, the United States sent the first living creatures to orbit the Earth—fruit flies. These tiny astronauts traveled aboard a V-2 rocket, and their mission was to help scientists understand the effects of space travel on living organisms, paving the way for future manned space missions.

310. A day on Mars, known as a sol, is only slightly longer than Earth's, lasting about 24 hours and 39 minutes. This similarity in day length makes Mars an intriguing subject for human exploration and potential future colonization.

311. Valles Marineris on Mars is the largest canyon in the solar system. This colossal canyon system stretches over 2,500 miles (4,000 kilometers) long and can reach depths of up to 7 miles (11 kilometers), dwarfing any canyon found on Earth.

312. The Helix Nebula, often called the "Eye of God," is a planetary nebula approximately 700 light-years away. Its appearance resembles a giant eye, making it one of the most visually striking and closest nebulae visible from Earth.

313. The Sun dominates our solar system, comprising 99.86% of its total mass. The remaining 0.14% is mainly contained within the planets, with Jupiter holding most of this residual mass. This illustrates the Sun's immense gravitational influence.

314. Ceres is the largest asteroid in the solar system and is also classified as a dwarf planet. It is located in the asteroid belt between Mars and Jupiter and has a diameter of about 590 miles (940 kilometers), making it a significant object of interest in planetary science.

315. Venus is the most volcanic planet in our solar system, boasting over 1,600 significant volcanoes. This volcanic activity contributes to Venus's extreme surface conditions and unique geological landscape.

316. The Oort Cloud is a theoretical cloud of icy bodies believed to surround the solar system at a distance of up to 100,000 astronomical units (AU) from the Sun. It is considered the source of long-period comets that occasionally enter the inner solar system.

317. HD 189733b, a planet located 63 light-years away, experiences some of the most extreme weather known, with winds of 4,500 mph (7,242 km/h) and rain made of molten glass. These conditions create a hellish environment, showcasing the diversity of planetary atmospheres.

318. A "light-year" is a measure of distance, not time. It represents the distance light travels in one year, approximately 5.88 trillion miles (9.46 trillion kilometers). This demonstrates the vast scales involved in astronomical measurements.

319. Neutron stars can spin at incredible speeds, with some known as pulsars rotating up to 716 times per second. These rapidly spinning stars emit beams of radiation that can be detected from Earth, providing insights into the extreme physics of collapsed stellar remnants.

320. The coldest temperature ever recorded in the universe is -457.6 degrees Fahrenheit (-272 degrees Celsius), measured in the Boomerang Nebula. This temperature is just a fraction above absolute zero, illustrating the extreme conditions present in space.

321. A space suit costs about $12 million, with the most expensive components being the backpack and control module. These suits are essential for protecting astronauts from the harsh conditions of space, ensuring their safety during extravehicular activities.

322. Neptune's largest moon, Triton, has a unique retrograde orbit, meaning it orbits the planet in the opposite direction of Neptune's rotation. This unusual orbit suggests that Triton was likely captured by Neptune's gravity rather than forming alongside the planet.

323. Jupiter's Great Red Spot is a massive storm raging for at least 400 years. This storm is so large that it could encompass three Earths, demonstrating the gas giant's immense and dynamic weather systems.

324. The universe is approximately 13.8 billion years old, a figure determined by studying cosmic microwave background radiation and its expansion rate. This age provides a timeline for the evolution of cosmic structures and the history of the cosmos.

325. The Soviet Union's launch of Sputnik 1 in 1957 marked the beginning of space exploration. This first artificial satellite's success ignited the space race between the United States and the Soviet Union, leading to significant advancements in space technology.

326. The Andromeda Galaxy is on a collision course with the Milky Way, moving toward our galaxy at about 110 kilometers per second (68 miles per second). This galactic collision is predicted to occur in about 4.5 billion years, forming a new galaxy.

327. Astronomers have discovered over 4,000 exoplanets, planets that orbit stars outside our solar system. The discovery of these distant worlds has expanded our understanding of planetary systems and the potential for habitable environments beyond Earth.

328. The Moon gradually moves away from Earth at about 1.5 inches (3.8 centimeters) per year. This gradual separation is caused by tidal interactions between the Earth and the Moon, affecting their mutual gravitational influence.

329. Rogue planets do not orbit any star and float freely through space. These lonely wanderers are scattered throughout the galaxy, offering unique challenges and opportunities for astronomical study.

330. Venus experiences no significant seasonal changes due to its nearly perfect circular orbit and slow rotation. This results in relatively constant temperatures across the planet, distinguishing its climate from the seasonal variations seen on Earth.

331. Voyager 1, launched in 1977, is the farthest human-made object from Earth. Currently, over 14 billion miles (22 billion kilometers) away, it continues to transmit data back to Earth as it travels through interstellar space.

332. There is a giant cloud of alcohol in space near the constellation Aquila. This cloud contains enough ethyl alcohol to supply every human on Earth with 300,000 pints of beer daily for a billion years, showcasing the surprising and diverse chemistry found in the universe.

As we conclude our journey through the wonders of the universe, we've marveled at the vastness of space and the incredible celestial bodies that inhabit it. From the twinkling stars to the enormous galaxies, the mysteries of the cosmos have shown us just how vast and extraordinary our universe truly is. But our exploration doesn't stop with the stars; there are wonders to be discovered right here on Earth as well.

Moving from the boundless expanse of space, we now turn our attention to the equally fascinating world of human innovation. Just as the universe is filled with awe-inspiring phenomena, our planet is brimming with incredible inventions that have transformed the way we live. These creations, born from the minds of inventive individuals, have revolutionized communication, transportation, medicine, and more, shaping the modern world in ways that were once unimaginable.

Our journey from the stars to the world of inventions highlights the endless curiosity and ingenuity of the human spirit. Just as astronomers and scientists strive to unlock the secrets of the universe, inventors and innovators push the boundaries of what is possible here on Earth. By exploring the coolest inventions that have changed our lives, we'll see how human creativity continues to drive progress and make our world a better place.

So, as we transition from the wonders of space to the marvels of human innovation, get ready to be inspired by the amazing creations that have shaped our lives. From everyday gadgets to groundbreaking technologies, the next chapter of our adventure will showcase the power of invention and the incredible impact it has on our world. Let's dive into the world of cool inventions and discover the ingenuity that continues to propel us forward.

Cool Inventions

Hey there, young innovators! Get ready to dive into the amazing world of inventions that have transformed the way we live. From the gadgets we use every day to groundbreaking technologies that push the boundaries of what's possible, innovation is all around us. In this chapter, we'll explore some of the coolest inventions that have shaped our world and discover how these incredible creations came to be.

Imagine life without your favorite gadgets – no smartphones, no computers, and no video games. It's hard to picture, right? These everyday devices have revolutionized how we communicate, learn, and have fun. We'll take a closer look at the stories behind these inventions, uncovering the brilliant minds and creative processes that brought them to life. You might be surprised to learn how some of these gadgets started as simple ideas or even accidents!

But it's not just about the tech toys and devices we use at home. Innovations in transportation, medicine, and energy have made huge impacts on our lives, making the world more connected and improving our quality of life. Think about cars that drive themselves, robots that perform surgeries, and renewable energy sources like solar and wind power. These groundbreaking technologies show the incredible potential of human ingenuity and creativity.

Have you ever wondered how inventions come to life? The journey from an idea to a finished product is often filled with challenges, setbacks, and moments of inspiration. We'll explore the exciting process of inventing, from brainstorming and prototyping to testing and refining. Along the way, you'll meet some of the most famous inventors in history and learn about their remarkable contributions to the world.

One of the most exciting aspects of studying inventions is realizing that innovation never stops. New ideas are being developed every day, and the future holds even more amazing possibilities. Who knows? Maybe one day, you'll come up with an invention that changes the world! By understanding the history and impact of past inventions, we can be inspired to think creatively and push the boundaries of what's possible.

So, get ready to be amazed by the coolest inventions that have changed our lives. From the simple gadgets we use every day to the groundbreaking technologies that shape our world, this journey through the world of innovation will open your eyes to the power of human creativity. Let's explore the incredible world of inventions and see how they continue to shape our lives and our future!

333. The first email was sent by Ray Tomlinson to himself in 1971. As a computer engineer, Tomlinson used the ARPANET system to send the first email message. This groundbreaking innovation laid the foundation for modern email communication, revolutionizing how we connect and share information. The content of that first email was a test message, likely something as simple as "QWERTYUIOP."

334. The microwave oven was invented after a researcher walked by a radar tube and a chocolate bar melted in his pocket. Percy Spencer, an engineer at Raytheon, noticed this phenomenon and realized microwaves could heat food. In 1945, he built the first microwave oven, which was initially large and expensive but eventually became a household staple, transforming cooking practices worldwide.

335. The first webcam monitored a coffee pot at the University of Cambridge. In 1991, researchers set up a camera to monitor the coffee levels in their lab's communal pot. This early webcam allowed them to check if coffee was available without leaving their desks, demonstrating the potential of video streaming technology for practical, everyday use.

336. A dentist invented the electric chair. In the late 19th century, Alfred P. Southwick, a dentist from Buffalo, New York, proposed the electric chair as a more humane method of execution compared to hanging. His background in dentistry helped him understand the principles of electrical currents and their effects on the human body, leading to the development of this execution method, which was first used in 1890.

337. The first alarm clock could only ring at 4 a.m. Invented by Levi Hutchins in 1787, this early alarm clock was designed solely to wake him up for work. It had a fixed mechanism that rang at 4 a.m. every day. The concept of adjustable alarm clocks came later, allowing people to set their preferred wake-up times, significantly improving personal scheduling and time management.

338. There are more than 1 million patents for computer-related inventions. Since the advent of computing technology, inventors and innovators have created various devices, software, and methods that have transformed industries and daily life. These patents cover everything from fundamental hardware components to advanced algorithms, reflecting the rapid pace of technological advancement and the continuous evolution of the field.

339. The first car accident occurred in 1891 in Ohio. James Lambert was driving one of his early gasoline-powered vehicles when he hit a tree root, lost control, and crashed into a hitching post. Both Lambert and his passenger were injured but survived. This incident highlighted the need for improved safety measures and regulations as automobiles began to populate the roads.

340. The first product with a barcode was Wrigley's gum. On June 26, 1974, a pack of Wrigley's Juicy Fruit gum became the first item ever scanned using a barcode at a supermarket in Troy, Ohio. This milestone marked the beginning of a new era in retail, enabling efficient inventory management and checkout processes. The adoption of barcodes revolutionized the global supply chain and retail industries.

341. The very first VCR, made in 1956, was the size of a piano. The Ampex VRX-1000, developed by Ampex Corporation, was the world's first practical videotape recorder. It used large reels of tape and was primarily used by television studios for recording and playback. Over time, VCR technology became more compact and affordable, eventually finding its way into households worldwide and changing how people consumed media.

342. The original design for Monopoly was circular. In 1904, Elizabeth Magie created the Landlord's Game to illustrate the economic consequences of land monopolies. The game featured a circular board and was intended to promote the ideas of Henry George, an economist advocating for a single tax on land value.

The concept later evolved into the rectangular board we know today, becoming one of history's most popular board games.

343. The first modern flushable toilet was invented by Sir John Harington in 1596. Harington, a godson of Queen Elizabeth I, designed a toilet with a cistern that flushed water to wash away waste. Although his invention was not widely adopted during his lifetime, it laid the groundwork for developing modern plumbing systems, greatly improving sanitation and public health.

344. Samuel Hopkins filed the first patent in 1790. Hopkins received the first U.S. patent for making potash, an essential ingredient in fertilizer. This event marked the beginning of the U.S. patent system, which encouraged innovation and provided inventors with legal protection for their creations. Today, the patent system promotes technological advancement and economic growth.

345. The inventor of Vaseline, Robert Chesebrough, ate a spoonful of it daily. In 1859, Chesebrough discovered the healing properties of petroleum jelly and began promoting it as a remedy for various ailments. To prove its safety and effectiveness, he famously consumed a spoonful of Vaseline daily and lived to 96, demonstrating his confidence in his product.

346. The first ice cream cone was made by a vendor at the 1904 World's Fair in St. Louis. Ernest Hamwi, a Syrian concessionaire selling zalabia (a type of waffle), helped out a neighboring ice cream vendor who had run out of dishes by rolling his waffles into cones. This innovative solution quickly caught on, and the ice cream cone became a popular treat, revolutionizing how ice cream was served and enjoyed.

347. The first computer mouse was made of wood. Invented by Douglas Engelbart in 1964, it was a simple, box-like device with two perpendicular wheels that tracked movement. Engelbart's invention revolutionized human-computer interaction, making navigating and controlling graphical user interfaces more accessible. The design has since evolved, but the basic concept remains a cornerstone of modern computing.

348. The first roller coaster was invented to distract Americans from sin. In the late 19th century, LaMarcus Thompson built the first roller coaster at Coney Island to provide a wholesome and thrilling alternative to the immoral activities he believed were corrupting American youth. His "Switchback Railway" quickly became popular, sparking the development of the amusement park industry and introducing generations to the joys of roller coasters.

349. The QWERTY keyboard was designed to prevent typewriter jams. Christopher Latham Sholes, the typewriter inventor, arranged the keys so that commonly used letter pairs were spaced apart to reduce the likelihood of mechanical jams. Despite developing more efficient alternatives, the QWERTY layout has persisted into the digital age, becoming the standard keyboard configuration for computers and other devices.

350. Bubble wrap was initially invented as wallpaper. In 1957, Alfred Fielding and Marc Chavannes created bubble wrap by sealing two shower curtains together, trapping air bubbles between them. Although it failed as a wallpaper material, they discovered its potential as a protective packaging material. Today, bubble wrap is widely used for cushioning fragile items during shipping and has become ubiquitous in the packaging industry.

351. The first commercial passenger flight lasted only 23 minutes. On January 1, 1914, Tony Jannus piloted a Benoist XIV biplane from St. Petersburg to Tampa, Florida, carrying one paying passenger. This inaugural flight marked the beginning of commercial aviation, demonstrating the potential for air travel to connect distant locations quickly and efficiently. The industry has since grown exponentially, revolutionizing global transportation.

352. The first bicycle, called a "swiftwalker," had no pedals. Invented by Karl von Drais in 1817, this early bicycle, known as the "draisienne" or "swiftwalker," required riders to push off the ground with their feet to propel themselves forward. The design

evolved, leading to the development of pedal-powered bicycles, which became a popular mode of transportation and recreation.

353. A banjo player invented Scotch tape. Richard Drew, a 3M engineer and banjo player, developed it in the 1920s. Initially designed as masking tape for automotive painting, the adhesive tape quickly found various uses in households and industries. Drew's invention has become indispensable for countless applications, from wrapping gifts to repairing torn paper.

354. A cartoon of President Theodore Roosevelt inspired the original Teddy bear. In 1902, political cartoonist Clifford Berryman depicted Roosevelt refusing to shoot a bear cub during a hunting trip. Inspired by this story, Morris Michtom, a Brooklyn shopkeeper, created a stuffed bear and named it "Teddy's Bear" in honor of the president. The toy became an instant success, leading to the widespread popularity of Teddy bears.

355. The first paper money was created in China 1,400 years ago. During the Tang Dynasty (618-907 AD), merchants and traders used promissory notes as a form of currency to avoid carrying heavy coins. This early form of paper money facilitated trade and commerce, eventually spreading to other parts of the world and revolutionizing the global economy.

356. The inventor of the Pringles can is now buried in one. Fred Baur, who developed the iconic Pringles can in 1966, was so proud of his invention that he requested to be buried in one. When he passed away in 2008, his family honored his wishes by placing a portion of his cremated remains in a Pringles can, highlighting his lasting legacy in the snack food industry.

357. The Guinness World Records book was created to settle bar bets. In the early 1950s, Sir Hugh Beaver, the managing director of the Guinness Brewery, was involved in a debate about the fastest game bird in Europe. Realizing that there was no reference book to settle such arguments, he commissioned the Guinness Book of World Records creation. Since its first publication in

1955, the book has become a global phenomenon, documenting extraordinary achievements and curiosities.

358. Writing was invented around 3400 BC in Mesopotamia by the Sumerians, who developed one of the earliest known systems of writing, cuneiform. This script involved pressing wedge-shaped marks into clay tablets, enabling the recording of transactions, laws, and stories and laying the foundation for written communication and historical record-keeping.

359. The ancient Sumerians invented the wheel, one of humanity's most transformative inventions, around 3500 BC. Initially used for pottery making, the wheel's application eventually extended to transportation and machinery, revolutionizing these fields and profoundly impacting civilizations' development.

360. Konrad Zuse invented the first programmable computer, the Z3, in 1941. This electromechanical computer utilized binary floating-point arithmetic, representing a critical milestone in the evolution of modern computing and paving the way for subsequent advancements in computer technology.

361. Thomas Edison invented the phonograph in 1877, marking the first device to play recorded sound. Edison's groundbreaking invention allowed people to listen to music and other audio recordings in their homes, fundamentally changing how people experienced entertainment.

362. Tim Berners-Lee's invention of the World Wide Web in 1989 revolutionized communication by enabling the global sharing of information via the Internet. This innovation transformed how people access, share, and interact with information, fundamentally altering daily life and work.

363. Chuck Hull created the first 3D printer in 1984, introducing a technology known as stereolithography. This revolutionary invention has since advanced, allowing for the creation of a wide range of items, from prototypes to prosthetics, significantly impacting manufacturing and medical fields.

364. The invention of the light bulb is often attributed to Thomas Edison. In 1879, Edison improved upon earlier designs to create a practical version suitable for widespread use. Edison's innovation was instrumental in electrifying cities and transforming urban life and industry.

365. Alexander Graham Bell invented the telephone in 1876, forever changing communication by allowing people to speak with each other over long distances. Bell's invention laid the groundwork for the global telecommunications industry, influencing countless aspects of modern society.

366. Carl von Linde's invention of the first practical refrigerator in 1876 revolutionized food storage by drastically reducing spoilage and improving public health. This innovation profoundly impacted daily life, food preservation, and the global food industry.

367. László Bíró invented the ballpoint pen in 1938, enhancing earlier designs with fast-drying ink that didn't smudge. Bíró's invention made writing more convenient and reliable, becoming a ubiquitous tool in business, education, and personal communication.

368. Christopher Latham Sholes invented the first practical typewriter in 1868, significantly improving the efficiency of written communication. Sholes' invention transformed business operations and personal correspondence, laying the foundation for modern typing devices.

369. The Wright brothers' creation of the first successful airplane, the Wright Flyer, in 1903 marked the beginning of modern aviation. This groundbreaking invention transformed global travel and commerce, opening up new possibilities for transportation and connectivity.

370. Joseph Nicéphore Niépce took the first successful photograph in 1826 using heliography. Niépce's pioneering work paved the way for the development of photography, a medium that has

since become essential for documenting and sharing the visual world.

371. John Henry Holmes invented the electric light switch in 1884. This simple yet transformative device allowed people to control electric lighting easily. This innovation contributed to the widespread adoption of electric light, enhancing safety and convenience in homes and workplaces.

372. The first mechanical clock, invented by monks in the 13th century, was crucial for regulating daily schedules and advancing scientific understanding of time. These early clocks played an essential role in the development of timekeeping and the coordination of communal activities.

373. Johannes Gutenberg's invention of the printing press in the 15th century revolutionized information dissemination. By making books more accessible, Gutenberg's press facilitated widespread literacy and the spread of knowledge, significantly impacting education and culture.

374. Gideon Sundback invented the first modern zipper in 1913, improving upon earlier designs to create a more reliable and functional fastener. Sundback's invention became the basis for contemporary zippers, which are now integral to clothing and accessories.

375. Leo Baekeland's invention of Bakelite, the first synthetic plastic, in 1907 marked the beginning of the modern plastics industry. Baekeland's innovation profoundly impacted manufacturing and everyday life, leading to the development of countless plastic products.

376. The first electronic digital computer, ENIAC, built in 1945 by John Presper Eckert and John Mauchly, calculated artillery trajectories during World War II. ENIAC's development was a significant milestone in computing history, influencing the future of electronic digital computers.

377. Thomas Crapper perfected the modern flush toilet in the 19th century, improving its efficiency and sanitation. While he did not invent the flush toilet, Crapper's enhancements made it more practical for everyday use, contributing to better public health standards.

378. The first commercially available cell phone, the Motorola DynaTAC 8000X, released in 1983, laid the groundwork for the mobile communication revolution. This pioneering device set the stage for the development of modern smartphones, transforming how people communicate and access information.

379. Wilson Greatbatch invented the pacemaker in 1960, a life-saving device that helps regulate heartbeats. Since its introduction, the pacemaker has saved countless lives, becoming a critical tool in cardiac care and medical technology.

380. Garrett Morgan invented the modern traffic light in 1923, introducing a design that included a "warning" light in addition to "stop" and "go" signals. Morgan's invention significantly improved road safety, reducing accidents and enhancing traffic flow in urban areas.

381. The U.S. Department of Defense developed the first GPS in the 1970s. Initially intended for military use, GPS technology has since become an essential tool for navigation and mapping in civilian life, revolutionizing how people travel and locate places.

As we wrap up our exploration of the coolest inventions that have transformed our lives, we see the incredible power of human creativity and innovation. From the gadgets we use every day to groundbreaking technologies that shape our world, these inventions showcase the limitless potential of the human mind. But our journey of discovery doesn't end here. Next, we turn our attention to another exciting aspect of human culture that brings people together and tests our abilities: the world of sports and games.

Just as inventions have revolutionized the way we live, sports and games have played a significant role in shaping our societies. They provide not only entertainment and excitement but also opportunities for teamwork, strategic thinking, and personal growth. Whether it's the thrill of scoring a goal or the satisfaction of a well-played game of chess, sports and games offer unique experiences that enrich our lives.

Moving from the realm of technological marvels, we now delve into the vibrant world of physical and mental challenges. Sports and games have a rich history, full of fascinating stories and cultural significance. They unite people across the globe, transcending language and borders, and fostering a sense of community and shared enjoyment. As we explore different sports and games, we'll see how they reflect the diverse ways people find joy, challenge themselves, and connect with others.

So, as we transition from the wonders of human invention to the excitement of sports and games, get ready to be inspired once again. This next chapter will highlight the dynamic and engaging activities that have captivated people for centuries and continue to bring us together today. Let's dive into the world of sports and games and discover the fun, history, and spirit of competition that make them an essential part of our lives.

Sports and Games

Hey there, future athletes and game enthusiasts! Get ready to dive into the thrilling world of sports and games. From the roar of the crowd in a packed stadium to the quiet concentration of a chess match, sports and games bring people together and test our skills, strength, and strategy. In this chapter, we'll explore a variety of sports, uncover their rich histories, and discover the fun games that people play all around the globe.

Imagine the rush of scoring the winning goal in a soccer match or the exhilaration of crossing the finish line in a race. Sports are more than just physical activities; they are a way for us to challenge ourselves, work as a team, and strive for excellence. We'll learn about popular sports like basketball, tennis, and swimming, and find out what makes each one unique and exciting.

But it's not all about the physical feats. Games like chess, board games, and video games require sharp minds and quick thinking. These games have fascinating origins and have evolved over time, becoming beloved pastimes for people of all ages. We'll explore the strategies and skills involved in these games and discover how they bring joy and entertainment to millions.

Did you know that some sports and games have been played for thousands of years? From the ancient Olympic Games in Greece to traditional games in different cultures, the history of sports is full of interesting stories and surprising facts. By looking back at the origins of these activities, we can appreciate how they have shaped cultures and brought people together throughout history.

One of the best parts of sports and games is that they can be enjoyed by everyone, regardless of age or ability. Whether you're playing a casual game of tag with friends or competing in an organized league, the joy of playing and the thrill of competition are universal experiences. We'll highlight some lesser-known sports and games from around the world, showing that there's something for everyone to enjoy.

So, lace up your sneakers, grab your game pieces, and get ready for an exciting adventure into the world of sports and games. From learning new sports to discovering fun games, this chapter will inspire you to get active, think strategically, and have a blast. Let's jump into the action and explore the incredible world of sports and games together!

382. The longest tennis match lasted over 11 hours. In 2010, John Isner and Nicolas Mahut played a historic match at Wimbledon

that spanned three days and lasted 11 hours and 5 minutes. The final set alone took 8 hours and 11 minutes, with Isner emerging victorious. This marathon match highlighted the physical and mental endurance required in professional tennis and set records for the longest match in terms of time and number of games played.

383. Golf balls were originally made of leather and feathers. Known as "featheries," these early golf balls were handcrafted by stuffing wet goose feathers into a leather pouch and stitching it closed. As the feathers dried, they expanded, creating a hard, durable ball. Featheries were used until the mid-19th century when they were replaced by gutta-percha balls, which were cheaper to produce and more consistent in performance.

384. Soccer is the most popular sport globally, with over 4 billion fans. Also known as football outside the United States, soccer's global appeal is due to its simplicity, accessibility, and excitement. With professional leagues and tournaments in virtually every country, soccer unites people of all ages and backgrounds, making it the world's most widely played and watched sport.

385. The first recorded Olympic Games took place in 776 BC. These ancient games were held in Olympia, Greece, and featured only one event: a 192-meter footrace called the Stadion. Over time, the games expanded to include a variety of athletic competitions, including wrestling, boxing, and equestrian events. The Olympic tradition was revived in the modern era, with the first modern Olympic Games held in Athens in 1896, continuing the legacy of athletic excellence.

386. The Stanley Cup has been around longer than the NHL. Donated in 1892 by Lord Stanley of Preston, it was originally awarded to Canada's top amateur hockey team. In 1926, it became the championship trophy for the National Hockey League (NHL). The Stanley Cup's rich history and tradition of engraving the names of winning team members make it one of the most coveted trophies in professional sports.

387. The first basketball game was played with a soccer ball and two peach baskets. Invented by Dr. James Naismith in 1891, it was initially created to keep his students at the International YMCA Training School in Springfield, Massachusetts, active during the winter months. The original rules and equipment have evolved significantly, but the game's core elements remain unchanged.

388. The first official baseball game was played in 1846. On June 19, 1846, the Knickerbocker Base Ball Club faced the New York Nine at the Elysian Fields in Hoboken, New Jersey. The New York Nine won the game 23-1. This early match laid the groundwork for the development of modern baseball, which has since become America's pastime and a beloved sport worldwide.

389. The World Series has been held annually since 1903, except for 1904 and 1994. The 1904 World Series was canceled due to a dispute between the American and National Leagues, while the 1994 series was called off due to a players' strike. Despite these interruptions, the World Series remains one of the most prestigious and eagerly anticipated events in professional sports, showcasing the best teams in Major League Baseball.

390. The longest-recorded baseball game lasted 33 innings. On May 1, 1920, the Brooklyn Robins and the Boston Braves played a marathon game that ended in a 1-1 tie due to darkness. The game took 8 hours and 22 minutes to complete, setting records for the longest game by innings in Major League Baseball history. This epic contest demonstrated the endurance and determination of the players involved.

391. The sport of badminton was initially called "Poona." Developed in British India during the 19th century, the game was named after the city of Pune (formerly Poona). British officers stationed in India brought the game back to England, where it gained popularity. This was renamed badminton after Badminton House, the Duke of Beaufort's estate, where the game was played.

392. In 1963, Major League Baseball pitcher Gaylord Perry said they'd put a man on the moon before he'd hit a home run. On July 20, 1969, just hours after the Apollo 11 moon landing, Perry hit his first and only career home run. This coincidental timing added a humorous and historic twist to Perry's prediction, highlighting the unpredictability and charm of baseball.

393. The term "soccer" originated in England. While most of the world refers to the sport as football, the term "soccer" is derived from an abbreviation of "association football," distinguishing it from other forms of football, such as rugby. The term was widely used in England during the late 19th and early 20th centuries before falling out of favor in favor of "football."

394. The longest recorded boxing match lasted 110 rounds. On April 6, 1893, Andy Bowen and Jack Burke fought in New Orleans for 7 hours and 19 minutes. The bout was declared a no-contest after both fighters were too exhausted to continue. This grueling match highlighted the extreme physical demands of boxing and led to changes in the sport's rules to ensure the safety and well-being of the athletes.

395. The Olympic flag was created in 1913. Designed by Pierre de Coubertin, the flag features five interlocking rings representing the five inhabited continents of the world (Africa, the Americas, Asia, Europe, and Oceania). The colors of the rings—blue, yellow, black, green, and red—along with the white background were chosen because every national flag in the world includes at least one of these colors. The flag symbolizes the unity and diversity of the global Olympic movement.

396. A baseball game has 18 minutes of total action. While a typical Major League Baseball game lasts about three hours, the actual time spent playing with the ball is around 18 minutes. The rest of the time follows pitching changes, between-inning breaks, and other pauses. Despite this, baseball's strategic and suspenseful nature keeps fans engaged throughout the game.

397. A professional basketball game has more than 47 minutes of action. Unlike baseball, basketball features continuous play with few interruptions. A standard NBA game consists of four 12-minute quarters, totaling 48 minutes of action. The fast-paced nature of the sport, combined with frequent scoring and dynamic plays, makes basketball an exciting and engaging experience for fans.

398. The Tour de France bicycle race is more than 100 years old. First held in 1903, it is one of the world's most prestigious and grueling cycling races. The multi-stage race covers approximately 3,500 kilometers (2,200 miles) over three weeks, challenging riders with various terrains, including mountains, flat stages, and time trials. The race's rich history and intense competition make it a highlight of the international sporting calendar.

399. The first women's Olympic Games were held in 1922 in Paris. Known as the Women's World Games, this event was organized by French athlete Alice Milliat in response to the exclusion of women from many Olympic events. The success of these games helped pave the way for greater inclusion of women in the Olympic movement, leading to the gradual expansion of women's events in subsequent Olympic Games..

400. Wrestling is the oldest competitive sport, dating back to ancient civilizations. It is one of the oldest known sports. It was a prominent event in the ancient Olympic Games and has been practiced in various forms worldwide. Wrestling's long history and enduring popularity highlight its fundamental appeal as a test of strength, skill, and strategy.

401. A soccer ball is made of 32 leather panels. Traditionally, soccer balls were constructed with 32 hexagonal and pentagonal leather panels stitched together to form a spherical shape. This design provides durability and a consistent flight pattern. Modern soccer balls may use different materials and construction techniques, but the classic 32-panel design remains iconic.

402. The first Winter Olympic Games were held in 1924 in Chamonix, France. Originally known as the "International Winter Sports Week," the event featured six sports and 16 events. The success of these games led to the establishment of the Winter Olympics as a regular event held every four years. The Winter Games have grown to include a wide range of sports, showcasing the skills and talents of athletes worldwide.

403. Ping-pong is the world's most popular indoor sport. Also known as table tennis, it is played by millions of people globally. Its popularity is due to its accessibility—requiring minimal equipment and space—and its fast-paced, skillful gameplay. The sport has a rich competitive history, with international tournaments and a strong presence in the Olympic Games, further cementing its status as a beloved and widely played sport.

404. American football was invented in the 19th century, evolving from rugby and soccer. The game developed unique rules and a distinct playing style, leading to its first official match in 1869. This historic game between Rutgers and Princeton marked the beginning of one of America's most popular sports.

405. On the other hand, Rugby has its roots dating back to 1823 at Rugby School in England. The sport is said to have originated when a student named William Webb Ellis defied the norms of a soccer game by picking up the ball and running with it. This bold move laid the foundation for rugby, which soon developed its own set of rules and traditions.

406. Soccer, or football as it is known outside the United States, was officially codified in England in 1863. The formation of the Football Association in London played a crucial role in standardizing the game's rules, effectively distinguishing it from rugby. This codification helped soccer become the globally beloved sport it is today.

407. The first Super Bowl, a milestone in American sports history, was played on January 15, 1967. In this inaugural National Football League (NFL) championship game, the Green Bay

Packers triumphed over the Kansas City Chiefs. The Super Bowl has become one of the world's most popular sporting events.

As we transition from the vibrant world of sports and games, where excitement and strategy play key roles, we find ourselves at the starting line of another thrilling journey. Just as sports and games captivate us with their unique challenges and histories, the world of cars offers a similar allure with its blend of speed, innovation, and fascinating stories. From the roar of engines on a racetrack to the timeless elegance of classic automobiles, cars have a way of igniting our passion and curiosity.

Moving from the fields and courts to the open roads and race tracks, we will explore the many facets of automotive marvels. Just like the variety of sports and games that cater to different interests and skills, cars come in an array of styles and purposes, each with its own unique charm. Whether it's the precision engineering of a high-speed race car or the nostalgic beauty of a vintage classic, the world of cars is filled with stories that parallel the excitement and diversity we've seen in sports and games.

As we shift gears from the spirit of competition and play to the thrill of the open road, get ready to discover the fascinating world of cars. This next chapter will take us on a journey through the fast, the old, the slow, and everything in between, revealing interesting facts and captivating tales that highlight the innovation and passion behind these incredible machines. So, let's buckle up and explore the exciting world of cars together!

Super Speed Vehicles

Hey there, young car enthusiasts and speed lovers! Get ready to buckle up and dive into the thrilling world of cars. From the fastest sports cars that zoom down the track to the oldest classic cars that have a rich history, there's so much to learn and explore. In this chapter, we'll discover the excitement of all kinds of cars, uncovering interesting facts that make each one unique.

Imagine the roar of an engine as a race car speeds by, or the sleek design of a luxury car gliding down the road. Cars are not just a means of transportation; they are marvels of engineering and design that capture our imagination and ignite our passion. We'll explore some of the fastest cars in the world, learning about their incredible speeds and the technology that makes them so quick.

But speed isn't the only fascinating aspect of cars. Some of the oldest cars tell amazing stories about the early days of automotive history. We'll take a journey back in time to discover how cars have evolved from simple, early models to the advanced vehicles we see today. You'll be amazed by the creativity and innovation that have driven the automotive industry forward over the years.

Cars come in all shapes and sizes, from tiny compact cars to massive trucks. Each type of car serves a different purpose and has its own set of interesting features. We'll look at the variety of cars on the road and learn about the unique characteristics that make them special. Whether it's the durability of a rugged off-road vehicle or the efficiency of a hybrid car, there's something fascinating about each one.

Did you know that some cars are designed to be incredibly slow and steady, while others are built for maximum speed? We'll explore these differences and find out why some cars are built for leisurely drives while others are made for the racetrack. Along the way, we'll uncover fun and surprising facts about cars that will fuel your curiosity and deepen your appreciation for these incredible machines.

So, get ready to hit the road and embark on an exciting adventure into the world of cars. From the fastest to the oldest, the slowest to the most innovative, this chapter will take you on a ride through the fascinating history and diverse world of automobiles. Let's discover the thrill of cars and the many interesting facts that make them so captivating!

408. The first speed limit for cars was set at 2 mph in cities and four mph in the countryside in the UK. A man walked in front of the vehicle, waving a red flag.

409. Some high-end cars in the 1950s and 1960s, like the Bond DB5 from "James Bond," featured ejector seats.

410. Many cars have "Easter eggs" or hidden features designed by the manufacturers. For example, some Jeep models have a tiny hidden image of a Jeep on the windshield.

411. The longest car ever built was a limousine measuring over 100 feet. It had 26 wheels and included a swimming pool and a helipad.

412. The smallest car ever made is the Peel P50, which is only 54 inches long and 39 inches wide.

413. Motorola introduced the first car radio in 1930, which led to the company's name (Motorola = Motor + Victrola).

414. The Rinspeed sQuba is a Swiss concept car that can drive both on land and underwater.

415. The first recorded automobile accident occurred in Ohio City, Ohio, in 1891.

416. Some cars can change colors. For example, BMW showcased a car with color-changing paint called the GINA Light Visionary Model.

417. The average car has about 30,000 parts and travels the equivalent of four times around the world in its lifetime.

418. The world's first electric traffic light was installed in Cleveland, Ohio 1914.

419. The "new car smell" comprises over 50 volatile organic compounds.

420. Tesla cars have a "fart mode" where the seats emit a fart sound, and "Romance Mode" that shows a fireplace on the screen and plays romantic music.

421. Armored cars have been used since World War I, and today's bulletproof cars can withstand grenades and bullets.

422. The ThrustSSC is the current land speed record holder, reaching 763 mph in 1997.

423. Modern car designs are often influenced by the shapes of fish and birds to improve aerodynamics.

424. Some BMW models can be parked using a remote control while the driver stands outside the car.

425. Contrary to popular belief, black motor oil doesn't necessarily mean it's dirty; it's just doing its job by holding the dirt in suspension.

426. Due to their silent operation, electric cars are often equipped with artificial sounds to alert pedestrians.

427. Many car brands, like Ford (Henry Ford) and Ferrari (Enzo Ferrari), are named after their founders.

428. Some modern cars have windshields that display information like speed and navigation directly on the glass.

429. Some car manufacturers have developed paint that can repair minor scratches when exposed to heat.

430. Some cars, like the Tesla Model S, feature panoramic glass roofs that give passengers a view of the sky.

431. The 1884 De Dion Bouton et Trepardoux Dos-a-Dos Steam Runabout is the oldest functioning car, which still runs on steam.

432. Several companies are developing flying cars, with prototypes like the Terrafugia Transition already taking test flights.

433. Some cars, like those in Formula 1, have steering wheels that are not circular but rectangular to improve control and visibility.

434. Some car alarms are programmed to emit the sound of a barking dog to deter thieves.

435. Formula E is a racing series for electric cars emphasizing sustainability and renewable energy.

436. In some places, carpool lanes are open to hybrid and electric vehicles regardless of the number of passengers.

437. Over 95% of a car can be recycled, and the steel from old cars is often used to make new vehicles.

As we wrap up our exhilarating journey through the world of cars, with their incredible speeds, rich histories, and fascinating facts, we see how innovation and human ingenuity have shaped the vehicles we use today. But our quest for knowledge and amazement doesn't stop with automobiles. Just as cars have surprised and captivated us, the world is brimming with even more astonishing and unbelievable facts that will leave you in awe.

Moving from the engineering marvels of the automotive world, we now turn our attention to the broader spectrum of oddities and wonders that our planet has to offer. The realm of crazy but true facts is filled with stories and phenomena that challenge our understanding and spark our curiosity. Just as we marveled at the speed and design of cars, we will now explore the peculiar and mind-boggling aspects of nature, science, and human history.

This transition from the thrilling world of cars to the astonishing world of unbelievable facts highlights the endless surprises our world holds. Whether it's a fish that can walk on land or a historical event so strange it seems like fiction, these crazy but true facts will continue to inspire and amaze us. So, buckle up for another exciting adventure as we delve into the most astonishing and unbelievable facts that make our world a truly extraordinary place

Crazy but True

Hey there, future fact-finders and wonder-seekers! Get ready to uncover some of the most astonishing and unbelievable facts that are so crazy, you'll hardly believe they are true. Our world is full of oddities and wonders that can surprise even the most curious minds. In this chapter, we'll dive into the strange, the weird, and the absolutely amazing things that make our world such a fascinating place.

Imagine learning that there are animals that can live without their heads, or that there are places on Earth where it rains fish. These are not just wild tales but true stories that reveal the incredible diversity and mystery of our planet. We'll explore these unbelievable facts, each one more surprising than the last, showing you just how extraordinary the world around us can be.

Did you know that some trees can communicate with each other, or that there's a place in the world where gravity doesn't seem to work the way we expect? These mind-boggling facts will make you question everything you thought you knew about science and nature. We'll delve into the secrets of the natural world, uncovering the strange phenomena that defy explanation and leave us in awe.

But it's not just nature that holds amazing surprises. Human history is also filled with incredible and bizarre events that sound too strange to be true. From unbelievable coincidences to extraordinary achievements, we'll discover the odd and wonderful stories that highlight the quirky side of human nature. These tales will not only entertain you but also show you the endless possibilities of what can happen in our world.

One of the most exciting parts of uncovering crazy but true facts is the sense of wonder and curiosity they inspire. These astonishing tidbits remind us that there's always more to learn and discover, and that the world is full of surprises waiting to be found. By exploring these facts, we can ignite our imagination and develop a deeper appreciation for the extraordinary details of everyday life.

So, get ready to be amazed and astounded as we dive into the realm of the unbelievable. From the peculiarities of nature to the oddities of history, this chapter will take you on a journey through the most astonishing and unbelievable facts that are crazy but true. Prepare to have your mind blown and your curiosity sparked as we explore the wonders and oddities of our world together!

438. The longest hiccuping spree lasted 68 years. An American farmer, Charles Osborne, began hiccuping in 1922 and continued until 1990, hiccuping an estimated 430 million times. His

condition baffled doctors and defied treatment, but he managed to live a relatively everyday life despite the persistent hiccups.

439. The shortest war in history lasted 38 minutes. On August 27, 1896, the Anglo-Zanzibar War was fought between the United Kingdom and the Sultanate of Zanzibar. The conflict began when Sultan Khalid bin Barghash refused to step down after the death of the previous sultan. British forces quickly overpowered Zanzibar, resulting in a swift victory and the shortest recorded war in history.

440. Honey never spoils. Archaeologists have found honey pots in ancient Egyptian tombs that are over 3,000 years old and still edible. Honey's low water content and acidic pH create an inhospitable environment for bacteria and microorganisms, allowing it to remain preserved indefinitely. This remarkable longevity makes honey a unique and valuable natural food product.

441. You can't hum while holding your nose closed. Humming requires the passage of air through the nasal passages, creating vibrations that produce sound. When you close your nose, you block this airflow, making it impossible to hum. This simple yet curious fact demonstrates the interconnectedness of our respiratory and vocal systems.

442. A sneeze travels at about 100 miles per hour. The forceful expulsion of air during a sneeze propels droplets out of the nose and mouth at high speeds, potentially spreading germs over a wide area. This rapid release helps clear irritants from the nasal passages but also highlights the importance of covering your mouth and nose to prevent the spread of illnesses.

443. The inventor of the Frisbee was turned into a Frisbee after he died. Fred Morrison, who invented the Frisbee in 1948, requested that his ashes be incorporated into a batch of flying discs after he died in 2010. His family honored this request, creating a unique and fitting tribute to the man who popularized the iconic toy.

444. The average person will wait six months for red lights to turn green. This estimate highlights the significant time we spend daily on seemingly mundane activities. Traffic signals, while necessary for safety and order, contribute to the cumulative waiting time we experience over a lifetime.

445. The human nose can detect more than 1 trillion different scents. Thanks to the complex structure of the olfactory system, our sense of smell is incredibly sensitive. With around 400 olfactory receptors, the human nose can distinguish various odors, which are crucial in our perception of the environment, food, and emotions.

446. There are more stars in the universe than grains of sand on all the world's beaches. The observable universe contains an estimated 100 billion galaxies, each with billions of stars. This staggering number underscores the vastness and complexity of the cosmos, highlighting its immense scale and the potential for countless planetary systems and forms of life.

447. A single strand of spaghetti is called a "spaghetto." In Italian, "spaghetti" is the plural form of "spaghetto," which refers to a single piece of pasta. This linguistic detail highlights the importance of understanding the nuances of language, especially regarding the names of familiar foods and dishes.

448. The inventor of the Rubik's Cube took one month to solve the puzzle after creating it. A Hungarian architect and professor, Erno Rubik, invented the Rubik's Cube in 1974 as a teaching tool to explain three-dimensional geometry. After scrambling the cube for the first time, it took him about a month to figure out how to solve it. The puzzle has become one of history's best-selling and most challenging toys.

449. A strawberry isn't an actual berry, but a banana is. Botanically, strawberries are aggregate fruits, formed from multiple ovaries of a single flower. In contrast, bananas develop from a single ovary and contain seeds, classifying them as berries. This distinction challenges our shared understanding of fruit

classifications and highlights the diversity of plant reproductive strategies.

450. Only one letter doesn't appear in any U.S. state name: Q. Despite the diverse range of state names, the letter Q needs to be more present. This linguistic quirk highlights the variety and uniqueness of the names chosen for the 50 states, reflecting the cultural and historical influences that shaped them.

451. A single cloud can weigh more than a million pounds. Clouds are composed of tiny water droplets or ice crystals; despite their fluffy appearance, they contain a substantial amount of water. A typical cumulus cloud can weigh around 1.1 million pounds (500,000 kilograms), illustrating these atmospheric formations' impressive scale and density.

452. The average person walks a remarkable distance in their lifetime, equivalent to five times around the world. This estimation is based on the average daily steps taken and the typical life expectancy.

453. Adding to the marvels of our world, the largest snowflake ever recorded was discovered at Fort Keogh, Montana, in 1887. This gigantic snowflake measured an astounding 15 inches wide and 8 inches thick.

454. Interestingly, a "jiffy" is an actual unit of time in physics and electronics. It represents the interval between alternating power cycles, typically 1/60 or 1/50 of a second, depending on the electrical system used.

455. The term "banana republic" originated in the early 20th century when certain Central American countries fell under the sway of powerful banana companies. These corporations, like the United Fruit Company, wielded immense political and economic influence, often shaping the governance and policies of these nations to suit their interests. This term has since become synonymous with politically unstable countries heavily dependent on a single export commodity, particularly when

110

foreign businesses have significant control over the local government.

456. The longest traffic jam in history occurred in China in 2010, stretching over 60 miles and lasting 12 days on the Beijing-Tibet Expressway. This unprecedented congestion was primarily due to road construction and an influx of vehicles heading towards Beijing. The jam caused significant delays, with some drivers stuck for days, relying on roadside vendors for food and water.

457. During the Vietnam War, duct tape proved to be an unconventional yet life-saving tool for surgeons who used it to close wounds when they ran out of traditional medical supplies. This pragmatic approach highlighted the tape's versatility and strength, demonstrating its surprising effectiveness in emergencies.

458. At Microsoft's headquarters in Redmond, Washington, lies the world's quietest room, an anechoic chamber so silent that one can hear their organs functioning. This room is used to test electronic devices. It is so devoid of sound that the longest anyone can endure the silence is 45 minutes due to the overwhelming sensory deprivation it causes.

459. In Chestnut Ridge Park, New York, a unique natural phenomenon, Eternal Flame Falls, features a small waterfall with a natural gas leak. This gas leak sustains a small, perpetual flame behind the waterfall, creating a mesmerizing and rare sight where fire and water coexist.

460. The longest word in English is the chemical name for the protein titin, containing a staggering 189,819 letters. Pronouncing this word would take over three hours, reflecting the complex and extensive nature of scientific terminology used to describe large proteins.

461. In Venice, a centuries-old law mandates that gondolas be painted black, a regulation dating back to the 17th century. This law was established to prevent the wealthy from competing

through extravagant displays of gondola decoration, ensuring a uniform appearance for these iconic Venetian boats unless they belonged to a high-ranking official.

462. Derinkuyu, an underground city in Turkey, exemplifies ancient ingenuity and resilience. This subterranean metropolis built during the Byzantine era could house up to 20,000 people and featured amenities such as schools, stables, and storage rooms. It served as a refuge from invasions and natural disasters, showcasing the sophisticated engineering of its time.

463. The longest concert ever held in Canada in 2010 lasted an incredible 453 hours, 54 minutes, and 40 seconds. This marathon event featured a rotating roster of musicians, setting a record for endurance in musical performance and highlighting the communal spirit and dedication of the participants.

464. Blue streetlights have been installed in some areas of Japan to reduce crime rates. Studies have suggested that blue lighting can calm people, potentially deterring criminal behavior and promoting safety and tranquility in urban environments.

465. In Switzerland, it's illegal to own just one guinea pig. This law is in place because guinea pigs are highly social animals that thrive on interaction with others of their kind. When kept alone, they can experience loneliness and depression, which is why Swiss law mandates that they be kept in pairs or groups to ensure their well-being.

466. There are more possible iterations of a chess game than atoms in the known universe. This mind-boggling fact highlights chess's complexity and depth. Despite its seemingly straightforward rules, the number of potential game variations is astronomical, providing endless opportunities for strategy and creativity.

467. A small child could swim through the veins of a blue whale. Blue whales are the largest animals on Earth, with hearts that can weigh as much as a small car and arteries so large that a human

could theoretically swim through them. This fact illustrates the sheer scale of these magnificent creatures.

468. The inventor of the Pringles can, Fred Baur, is buried in one. When Baur passed away in 2008, part of his ashes were placed in a Pringles can at his request. This unusual burial choice honors his significant contribution to snack food packaging.

469. Scotland has 421 words for "snow." This extensive vocabulary reflects the importance and variability of snow in Scottish culture. Each word describes different types and conditions of snow, showcasing the richness of the Scots language.

470. There are more trees on Earth than stars in the Milky Way galaxy. With an estimated three trillion trees on our planet, their number far surpasses the estimated 100-400 billion stars in our galaxy. This fact underscores the abundance and diversity of Earth's forests.

471. Oxford University is older than the Aztec Empire. Founded in 1096, Oxford predates the establishment of the Aztec civilization, which began around 1325. This historical comparison highlights the enduring legacy of one of the world's oldest universities.

472. An apple, potato, and onion all taste the same if you eat them with your nose plugged. Our sense of taste is closely linked to our sense of smell. Without the ability to smell, the distinct flavors of these foods become indistinguishable, demonstrating the importance of olfactory input in tasting food.

473. A blob of toothpaste is called a "nurdle." This playful term refers to the dollop of toothpaste on your toothbrush. It's a small but essential part of daily oral hygiene routines.

474. A day on Pluto is about 153 hours long. This means that a single day on Pluto, from one sunrise to the next, lasts over six Earth days. This lengthy rotation period is due to Pluto's slow spin on its axis.

475. There's a museum in Iceland dedicated to penises. The Icelandic Phallological Museum houses a vast collection of penises and penile parts from various animals, including whales, seals, and land mammals. It's a unique and somewhat quirky museum that attracts curious visitors worldwide.

476. A single teaspoon of honey represents the life work of 12 bees. Bees work tirelessly to produce honey, and it takes the combined effort of many bees to create even a tiny amount. This fact highlights the incredible efficiency and cooperation within a bee colony.

477. Letting a sumo wrestler make your baby cry is good luck in Japan. This tradition is part of a sumo ritual where the wrestlers hold babies and try to make them cry. A crying baby is believed to bring good health, and There are more stars in the universe than grains of sand on all the Earth's beaches. With an estimated 100 billion galaxies, each containing millions to billions of stars, the total number of stars is mind-bogglingly large, far exceeding the number of sand grains on Earth.

478. Bananas glow blue under black lights. This phenomenon occurs due to the breakdown of chlorophyll in the peel, which produces a fluorescent compound. Under ultraviolet light, this compound emits a blue glow, revealing a hidden aspect of this everyday fruit.

479. There's a basketball court above the Supreme Court in the U.S. Known as the "Highest Court in the Land," located on the top floor of the U.S. Supreme Court Building. Court employees use it for recreational purposes, uniquely contrasting the serious judicial work below.

480. The shortest commercial flight in the world is in Scotland and lasts 1.5 minutes. This flight, operated by Loganair, travels between the islands of Westray and Papa Westray in the Orkney Islands. The flight covers just 1.7 miles, making it a unique and brief journey.

481. A duel between three people is called a "truel." Unlike a duel involving two participants, a truel involves three, adding complexity to the concept of a duel and requiring different strategic considerations.

482. Walt Disney was afraid of mice. Ironically, the creator of the world's most famous mouse, Mickey Mouse, had a fear of the very creatures that inspired his beloved character. This personal detail adds an interesting twist to Disney's legacy.

483. The inventor of Vaseline used to eat a spoonful of it every day. Robert Chesebrough, who discovered the substance in 1859, believed in its medicinal properties so strongly that he consumed it daily. This unusual habit underscores his confidence in the product he created.

484. In France, it's legal to marry a dead person. This practice is known as posthumous marriage, and it is allowed under French law if there is proof that the deceased intended to marry the living partner. This rare and poignant legal allowance demonstrates the flexibility of marriage laws in certain circumstances.

485. The longest time between two twins' births is 87 days. This extraordinary case occurred when one twin was born prematurely, and the mother was able to delay the birth of the second twin, resulting in a record-breaking gap between their births.

486. In 2006, a Coca-Cola employee offered to sell Coca-Cola secrets to Pepsi. Pepsi responded by notifying Coca-Cola, demonstrating the ethical standards upheld by the rival company. This act of corporate integrity prevented a potential breach of trade secrets.

487. The inventor of the pacemaker had a severe heart condition. Wilson Greatbatch, who created the first implantable pacemaker, suffered from heart problems himself. His personal experience likely fueled his dedication to developing this life-saving device.

488. A sheep, a duck, and a rooster were the first passengers in a hot air balloon. In 1783, the Montgolfier brothers launched a balloon carrying these animals to test the effects of flight. This pioneering experiment paved the way for human flight by demonstrating that living creatures could survive airborne travel.

489. There's a fruit that tastes like chocolate pudding: black sapote— also known as the "chocolate pudding fruit," black sapote has a creamy texture and sweet flavor that resembles chocolate, offering a natural and healthy alternative to dessert.

490. Some fungi create zombies and then control their minds. Certain parasitic fungi infect insects, taking over their nervous systems and controlling their behavior to ensure the spread of the fungal spores. This gruesome but fascinating interaction illustrates the complex relationships in nature.

491. There's a tree that can grow 40 different kinds of fruit. Known as the "Tree of 40 Fruits," it is created through grafting techniques and can produce various stone fruits, including peaches, plums, apricots, and cherries. This innovative horticultural project highlights the possibilities of plant grafting.

492. A small percentage of the static on "dead" TV stations is leftover radiation from the Big Bang. This cosmic microwave background radiation is a remnant of the early universe, providing a tangible connection to the origins of the cosmos and the Big Bang theory.

493. Bananas are naturally radioactive because they contain potassium-40, a naturally occurring isotope that emits small amounts of radiation

494. The world's longest limousine measures over 100 feet and comes equipped with a swimming pool, a helipad, and a king-sized bed

495. The first robot was created by Leonardo da Vinci in the 15th century, and it was designed to look like a knight that could sit, wave, and even open its visor

496. Venus rotates so slowly that a day on Venus is longer than a year on the planet; it takes 243 Earth days for Venus to complete one rotation but only 225 Earth days to orbit the Sun.

497. There is a river in Venezuela called the Catatumbo River that experiences lightning storms for about 260 nights a year, making it one of the most electrifying places on Earth.

498. The ancient city of Troy, made famous by the story of the Trojan War, was believed to be a myth until its ruins were discovered in Turkey in the 19th century.

499. The Micropachycephalosaurus, whose name means 'tiny thick-headed lizard,' is one of the smallest dinosaurs ever discovered, measuring only about 3 feet long.

500. Some species of frogs can freeze solid during winter and thaw back to life in the spring without any harm, thanks to natural antifreeze in their bodies.

Keep the Curiosity Alive

As you journed through the chapters of this book, you uncover the fascinating secrets and wonders of our world, from the curious creatures that share our planet to the colossal dinosaurs of the past and the vast mysteries of outer space.

Each page was designed to ignite your curiosity and fill your mind with fantastic facts that will leave you eager to learn more.

Keep in mind that curiosity is the catalyst for discovery. It's the driving force behind scientists, historians, and inventors, propelling them to venture into uncharted territories and unveil the concealed truths of our universe. By embracing your curiosity, you'll amass a wealth of 'aha!' moments and foster a profound admiration for the awe-inspiring world surrounding you.

To finish with a couple of final facts, once you have finished this book, you will have read 24303 words or 132,124 characters.

Afterword

Now that you have everything you need to amaze your friends with incredible facts and blow their minds with your newfound knowledge, it's time to pass on what you've learned and show other curious minds where they can find the same excitement and fun.

Simply by leaving your honest opinion of this book on Amazon, you'll show other young explorers where they can find the information they're looking for and pass on their passion for discovering cool and amazing facts.

Thank you for your help. The joy of learning is kept alive when we pass on our knowledge – and you're helping me to do just that.

Made in United States
Cleveland, OH
10 November 2024

10576824R00068